JESUS
FOR
A NO-GOD WORLD

JESUS
FOR
A NO-GOD WORLD

By
Neill Q. Hamilton

THE WESTMINSTER PRESS

Philadelphia

STANDARD BOOK No. 664–20857–6

LIBRARY OF CONGRESS CATALOG CARD No. 70–75457

BOOK DESIGN BY
DOROTHY ALDEN SMITH

PUBLISHED BY THE WESTMINSTER PRESS ®
PHILADELPHIA, PENNSYLVANIA
PRINTED IN THE UNITED STATES OF AMERICA

To the students whose vitality,
curiosity, and impatience have arrested
my complete obsolescence

CONTENTS

INTRODUCTION

Can the writing of another book related to Jesus really be excused? If there be any justification, it must arise out of the religious crisis of our time. I take this crisis to be our inability to state for our time what it means to believe in God and serve him.

In New Testament studies this crisis has stimulated the debate about demythologizing and, more recently, the new quest of the historical Jesus. Beyond the bounds of any one branch of theology the crisis has led to manifold attempts to restate the nature and mission of the church. Perhaps our dilemma has been most acute where we have tried to speak about ethics. Our frustration has reached the point where some are now suggesting that it would be wise to stop talking about "God" altogether until time heals the unfortunate reactions which that word evokes.

It may turn out that this last counsel will be the best. But before we take the vow of silence, one subject needs a larger airing—the doctrine of Christ. In the Christian tradition, statements about God depend upon statements about Christ. What better way, then, to explore more appropriate language about God than to seek more appropriate language about Christ? It is certain that we shall never talk sense of all the rest of Christianity until we talk sense of Christ.

The root conviction of this book is that New Testament tradition is richer with possibilities for making better sense about Christ than current debate has yet recognized. More particularly, this book will claim that the primitive Jewish Christian church had a way of speaking of Christ that could be especially helpful in our own cultural situation.

The difficulty about this early and most promising Christology is that it did not last long in its own day. It was soon overwhelmed by other Christologies serving other cultural necessities. Now it exists only in an obscure layer of tradition embedded in certain New Testament documents. Our task will be to expose this rich vein of tradition; describe it; see how and why it became obscured. When the Christology in question and its story are brought to light we can judge whether or not this hidden alternative deserves to be revived and become for us as live and refreshing an alternative as it once was.

The first three chapters describe what I take to be the chief elements in the burial story. The tension between Judaism and Hellenistic culture, the composition of stories of Jesus' ministry following the resurrection, and the separation of Christianity from Judaism all conspired to help cover what we now seek to expose.

The last two chapters describe this primitive Christology, how it served its originators, and how it might serve us.

The Christology in question is the one that interprets Jesus as the eschatological prophet.

The exploration of this Christology and its implications stretches from Cyrus, the Persian, to Johnson, the Texan. On such an extended journey I have paused for detailed discussion of any particular question only where, in my opinion, other research seems not to confirm my contentions or is not readily available. Of necessity, the result is more the illustration of a hypothesis than the demonstration of a case.

I

THE DAWN OF THE WORLD TO COME

The major adventure in contemporary Christian theology has been the attempt to create a theology for this world. From Bonhoeffer to Bishop Robinson's *Honest to God* to Cox's *The Secular City* and the no-God theologians, the common conviction is: this world has achieved such importance, maturity, and status that Christian thinkers must make it their primary concern. Among some theologians the world is a more important theme than God in the sense that if one has to choose, it is better to talk about the world and keep silent about God.

This is a curious but understandable twist of events. A careful regard for the empirical data of nature and history has rewarded man with understanding, control, and enjoyment of his situation in this world unparalleled in man's previous experience. But this has meant just as studious a disregard of the future world where tradition says God will reign. This world's gain has been the other world's loss. And God has gotten lost along with that world to come because tradition associates him primarily with the heavens. It is this traditional heavenly—or otherworldly—association of God that is the greatest obstacle to the creation of an adequate theology for our time.

This chapter aims to take the first step necessary to overcome this obstacle; namely, to recall how that world to come arose in the first place. Then we shall be in a better position to decide what to do with it. We may even come to realize in the light of its dawning that circumstances have so changed that it is time simply to let that other world go.

The trouble with Christian tradition is that it never advertises the fact that the future world was not always there. This is a way to shield us from doubt. But unless we are willing to test Christian tradition's firmest convictions we shall never be able to save that tradition from the prevailing doubt that the whole thing is becoming obsolete.

The next world is not the special property of Christianity. It was inherited from Judaism. It was no sudden creation. It emerged as the result of a long process that includes at least the periods when the Jewish people were Persian subjects and then subjects of Alexander the Great and his successors. The Persian period produced the presuppositions that prepared Israel for the doctrine of a world to come. The Hellenistic period saw a situation in Judaism that made adoption of that doctrine seem imperative.

The Persian Empire lasted for roughly two centuries. In 539 B.C. it defeated Babylon and replaced it as the dominant world power. Persian suzerainty in Palestine ended with the arrival there of Alexander the Great in 331 B.C. In the time between these two events, Judaism experienced the collapse of the prophetic interpretation of history. This failure of the prophetic movement cleared the way for the emergence of the heavenly world.

The idea of the failure of the prophetic movement is difficult for Christians to entertain. The conventional Christian view is that the prophetic movement was the crowning achievement of Israelite religion and that the "legalism" of Ezra and late Judaism was the result of Judaism's failure to appreciate what was best in its own heritage. But however difficult, history demands that we recognize that prophetism simply did not provide an adequate basis for the continuation of Judaism, fine as prophecy's contributions were. At the end of the prophetic period Israel was faced with the decision to find an alternative to the prophets or have its religion end with them!

We know that the absence of prophecy was a dogma of Maccabean times. (I Macc. 4:46; 9:27; 14:41.)[1] This may even have been the view in the time of Nehemiah, if his priest of the future with Urim and Thummim refers to a return of the gift of prophecy. (Neh. 7:64–65.)[2] When did the demise come?

The time of the end of the prophetic movement is easy to mark. Malachi, the last of the literary prophets, was written sometime in the first half of the fifth century B.C.[3] The author speaks of a divine messenger to precede the coming of the Lord for Final Judgment. Later an editor of the book equates the author with this messenger in the superscription he adds at Mal. 1:1. This editor still considers the prophetic movement alive and its predictions capable of immediate fulfillment. A later editor changes the identity of the messenger of ch. 3:1 to Elijah (ch. 4:5), working from the assumption that prophecy will not be fulfilled in historical fashion. Instead of a prophetic viewpoint he is using a late Jewish apocalyptic point of view which expects the return of some ancient prophet as a substitute. This second editor no longer expects that Israel is capable of producing prophets in the usual way. Prophecy will return only when God intervenes in history at the end. So it happened that the end of prophecy as a lively option came between the first and second editors of Malachi.

The prophetic movement collapsed because it failed to produce an adequate interpretation of Israel's experience in history. Things just did not work out the way the prophets of the Persian period claimed they should. The prophets in question are mainly Deutero-Isaiah, Trito-Isaiah, Haggai, Zechariah, and Malachi. A brief survey of their chief expectations will illustrate the point.[4]

Deutero-Isaiah was heir to certain prophetic traditions. The cardinal feature of his theory of history was that history is the unfolding of a previous prophetic message. But the weakness of this position was already being exposed in the necessity of Deutero-Isaiah to modify some of the traditions he inherited. According to one tradition, sovereignty over all the peoples of the earth was to be given to Israel by the reestablishment of God's anointed on the throne of David. He acknowledges this tradition in Isa. 55:3 but substitutes the whole people of Israel for David in v. 4. He is forced to some such modification because he sees that the throne will not come to an Israelite, let alone to a descendant of David. The actual anointed sovereign will be the Persian, Cyrus. By substituting Cyrus for David he repairs the prophecy that came to him. But his own explanation of what God is doing in history has no more success than the Davidic tradition.

For Deutero-Isaiah the main event in God's program of redemption was to be the return home of Israelite refugees from Babylon made possible by the Persian conquest of Babylon. The exiles were to be accompanied by Yahweh himself. The event was to include the same kind of miraculous signs that had attended the exodus, which is Deutero-Isaiah's model for redemption.

As a matter of historical fact this main event of the prophet's message did not come off. As Olmstead somewhat cynically points out, it was scarcely to be expected that Jews already rich would abandon fertile Babylonia for the barren hills of Judah.[5] Whatever the reason, there was no glorious return to Zion either of the exiles or of Yahweh.

(This criticism of Deutero-Isaiah does not do him full justice. It is beside the point of this survey to enumerate the enduring contributions of each prophet to the Jewish and Christian traditions. This would include in Deutero-Isaiah's case elements such as the hopeful character of his vision of redemption, the scope of his vision which included creation, and his penetrating insights into the redemptive role of man suffering. Our purpose here is to show one thing: each prophet failed to provide a viable explanation of the course of history for his time.)

Trito-Isaiah inherited the disillusionment of his predecessor's unfulfilled hopes. He was unable to make any comforting innovation. He simply but courageously repeated and reinforced the promise of Yahweh's advent to Jerusalem.[6]

Haggai and Zechariah carried forward the same promise but with an addition. They introduced a condition upon which the return of Yahweh depended. The Temple must first be rebuilt before God will come to establish his Kingdom.

The Persian government actually did provide for the building of the Temple, but Haggai was careful to exclude any such outsider from receiving credit along with God no matter what he contributed. Perhaps Haggai's exclusivistic attitude was partly based on hope of the breakup of the Persian Empire. Writing in the second year of Darius (520), he may have been encouraged by the widespread revolt going on at that time. In the process of Bardiya displacing Cambyses as king only to be displaced himself by Darius, the empire became so unsettled that in the first year of his reign Darius recorded revolts in Parsa, Elam, Media, Assyria, Egypt, Parthia, Sattagydia, and Saka.[7] For whatever reason, so confident was Haggai of a new chance of freedom for Judah that he took the unprecedented step of naming the promised anointed occupant-to-be of David's throne. He designated Zerubbabel, the grandson of Jehoiachin. Jeremiah had used a plucked-off ring to symbolize the rejection of Jehoiachin. Haggai used the same symbol for the divine appointment of the grandson:[8] "I will take you, O Zerubbabel my servant . . . , says the LORD, and make you like a signet ring" (Hag. 2:23).

Zechariah, Haggai's contemporary, supported the Temple project and the nomination of Zerubbabel with an equally open announcement of him as the "shoot," a play on the name Zerubbabel, "seed of Babylon." In the context of Haggai's and Zechariah's prophecies and disturbances actually existing in the empire, Zerubbabel's superior, Tattenai, governor of Across the River, challenged the authority for the construction of the Temple. Fortunately for the Temple project, the archives of Ecbatana produced the register roll of Cyrus' enabling decree.

There was, of course, no authorization for the promotion of Zerubbabel from rank of a third-class governor to the rank of an independent king, nor did that ever happen. Zerubbabel simply disappears from the record. In the following year Darius himself passed through Palestine on his way to settle affairs in Egypt. In all probability he put down the incipient revolt in Judah and executed Zerubbabel as an insurgent. Perhaps Zechariah referred to just such a suppression when he wrote, "For before those days there was no wage for man or any wage for beast, neither was there any safety from the foe for him who went out or came in; for I set every man against his fellow" (Zech. 8:10).[9]

The resulting loss of confidence in prophecy must have been enormous. Not only had Haggai and Zechariah been mistaken in their reading of history but they had almost brought the vengeance of the dominant world power upon the whole of the Jewish people. Perhaps the opposition of Joshua, the high priest, to Zerubbabel had made it possible to dissociate Joshua and the rest of the Jewish community from the rebellious faction. The memory of the Zerubbabel fiasco would long have deterred anyone from placing his own political career or the future of the Jerusalem community in the hands of prophets.

The author of Malachi represented the last brief spasm of the prophetic movement's claim to the religious leadership of the community. He mainly polemicized against abuses within the community. He did, however, repeat the promise of Yahweh's imminent coming but with his own innovation. The sudden advent of the Lord to his Temple was to be preceded by a heavenly messenger. As we have noted above, a later editor turned this messenger into a shadowy figure of late Jewish apocalyptic, who waits in heaven until the end of history arrives. In this fashion the prophetic movement was laid to rest with the comforting promise of its revival in some indefinite, eschatological future.

Religious leadership in the Jewish community then passed to other types altogether. Priestly lawyers like Ezra and Nehemiah undertook responsibility to preserve true religion and ensure the destiny of the people of God. For an interpretation of history in the fourth century, the prophets gave way to the Chronicler.[10] This new writer did not look at history as a place of potential upheaval where some great act of redemption would radically alter the circumstances of the devotees of Yahweh. His key to the understanding of Israel's history lay in the concept of retribution. Whoever transgressed the will of God expressed in the Torah always suffered while pious kings always enjoyed prosperity. The function of the prophets according to the Chronicler was to warn the wicked of the impending judgment of God. The culmination of Israel's history was not the national independence and geopolitical superiority of prophecy but rather the restoration of Temple and Law under Persian rule. Far from expecting a revival of the prophetic movement, the whole conception of the Chronicler showed that he wrote as if Persian rule was destined for eternity. The union between the altar in Jerusalem and the throne at Susa seemed to be natural and indestructible![11] However, before its end, the fourth century was to bear witness to both the eclipse of the prophetic understanding of history as well as its replacement by the Chronicler's understanding of history.

It is important to reiterate, before pressing on, that the prophetic movement made other contributions more lasting than its theory of history. Our theme requires that we emphasize the failure of this theory because this failure prepared the path for an alternate understanding of history that called for the creation of a second, future world. Even when we do turn to the teachings of the prophets which Christian scholars usually consider their chief and abiding contribution, just these teachings merely further illustrate that the prophetic explanation of history had reached the limit of its usefulness. We may take, for example, Gerhard von Rad's suggestion that Jeremiah and Ezekiel came to the fullest expression of their genius with the contention that Israel was completely incapable of obeying God's will.[12] The bright side of that judgment was a promise of a radically new operation of God upon men to give them new hearts capable of obeying or, according to Ezekiel's metaphor, to raise dead, dry bones to new life. To this, they and Deutero-Isaiah added the promise of a new covenant. However meaningful these ideas came to be to Christians in much later times, in the prophets' own times they were signs that the prophetic theory of history was approaching exhaustion. The main factors in their theory of history were God, historical environment, and man. If, in order to explain their interrelation, they found it necessary to change the constitution of one of these given factors (namely, man) before their theory would work, they are perilously close to confessing that they simply had no viable solution for the actual problem.

It was just such visions of extraordinary capabilities for man and marvelous events designed to replace the saving events of conventional history that anticipated the solution to history that would follow the Chronicler. The time was ripe for another world in which the failures and frustrations of ordinary history would be displaced by success and fulfillment.

Actually, this idea of a future world was already available to the Jewish people in Persian culture. It was more than available. Certain religious aspects of Persian culture were so congenial to Jewish culture that this new solution was in a position to commend itself.

The Persian Empire was a most impressive bearer of its culture. When Cyrus fulfilled the prophecy of Deutero-Isaiah to the extent that he removed the yoke of Babylon, he was king of the greatest empire yet known to history. It must have seemed no exaggeration in his time for him to proclaim, "I am Cyrus, king of the world . . . king of the four rims of the earth."[13] His epitaph read, "king of kings." Following the model of Assyrian organization, Cyrus divided the empire into twenty sections called satrapies, each larger than any previous kingdom. Submission to the central authority was ensured by excellent communication, annual inspection of each province by an agent of Cyrus. Also there was a secretary, finance officer, and commanding general in each province responsible directly to the king of kings. Subject peoples were encouraged to continue their native style of life. In return for loyalty and taxes paid, they received efficient and just government.

It was as friendly a regime as it was impressive. We have already alluded to Cyrus' decree authorizing the construction of the Temple in Jerusalem at his own expense. It was in the very first year of his reign, 538 B.C., that he decreed: "Concerning the house of God at Jerusalem, let the house be rebuilt, the place where sacrifices are offered and burnt offerings are brought; . . . let the cost be paid from the royal treasury. And also let the gold and silver vessels of the house of God, which Nebuchadnezzar took out of the temple that is in Jerusalem and brought to Babylon, be restored and brought back to the temple which is in Jerusalem, each to its place; you shall put them in the house of God." (Ezra 6:3–5.)

This confirmed Deutero-Isaiah's estimate of Cyrus as God's "anointed" (Isa. 45:1) and "shepherd" (Isa. 44:28). Interpreters of the Old Testament tend to underestimate the messianic role of Cyrus for Israel. In the light of what Cyrus accomplished for the community of Jerusalem as well as the whole of Judaism dispersed throughout the Persian Empire, it would be fair to say that he inaugurated an epoch in the history of Israel more effective for their long-term well-being than any epoch arranged by Israel's own political leaders before or since. This is not intended to belittle the vitality and creativity of Israel. Albright is certainly correct in rejecting the curious opinion that the Persian Empire created Judaism.[14] It would, I think, be fair to say that the Persian Empire provided the supportive atmosphere in which Israel could develop a durable style of life.

If Ezra is reckoned as the founder of Judaism, then the Persians must be given appropriate credit for their role. The royal rescript of Artaxerxes I, the Persian king at the time, enabled Ezra to reform the religious organization of Jerusalem according to "the law of the God of heaven."

The Persian central authority even provided a kind of arbitration of religious disputes between Jewish communities. The

incident of the destruction of the Jewish temple at Elephantine
on the upper Nile is a case in point. Egyptian priests successfully bribed the Persian governor to have the Jewish temple
there destroyed in 411 B.C. In the process of attempting to
arrange its reconstruction, the Jews at Elephantine appealed
to Jerusalem. But Jerusalem would not welcome a competing
temple. Next, an appeal was made to the Persian governors of
Judea and to the sons of the governor of Samaria. This resulted
in a compromise recommendation to the satrap of Egypt that
the Elephantine temple be rebuilt but not for animal sacrifices.
This would please the Egyptian priests who objected to animal
sacrifices and would satisfy Jerusalem by reducing the competitor to a status beneath the central sanctuary.[15]

The friendly relations between the Jews and Persian
authority are illustrated in the Chronicler's theory of history.
We have already noted that he was so satisfied with Persian
rule that he never expected any other situation for Judaism.
Accordingly the Chronicler advocated a pacifist dependence
upon the Lord and an abhorrence of military power.

It may well be that The Book of Jonah belonged in the
Persian period and had as its main purpose the rebuttal of the
particularistic attitude of most of the prophets of that time. If
this were the case, then Nineveh, the ancient capital of Assyria,
would be an archaic symbol for the Persian Empire. The Book
of Jonah found these foreigners more than friendly. They were
capable of a positive response to the word of Yahweh. This
suggests that the religious side of Persian culture may have
been in some way congenial to the religion of Israel. The
possibility is worth exploring.

We have already observed that Deutero-Isaiah and the
Chronicler considered Persian kings God's appointed guardians
of Israel. In fact there was an important monotheistic element
common to both the theologies of the Persian kings and the
theology of Israel due in large part to the religious creativity
of Zoroaster.

Zoroaster, a prophet who lived about 628–551 B.C.,[16] exercised his mission under the protection of King Vīshtāspa, whom he converted. Vīshtāspa was king of Chorasmia until that country was overthrown by Cyrus. Although Chorasmia was the place of his prophetic activity—an area that today includes Persian Khorasan, Western Afghanistan, and the Turkmen Republic of the Soviet Union—he may have been born in Media. Zoroaster is interesting not only because of the possible influence his religion and its variations had upon the Jews of his time but also because he is the one great creative religious genius which the Aryan race has produced.

Zoroaster proclaimed a single god, Ahura Mazdāh, which means "the wise Lord." The religious tradition around him posited many gods in two classes, daevas and ahuras. He dethroned the daevas, making them evil powers who refused to obey the wise Lord. He ignored all other ahuras with the clear result that Ahura Mazdāh alone was god.

It is easy to see in Zoroaster's doctrine of God themes common to Judaism. Like Yahweh he is the one God who created the world and operates in the world by his Holy Spirit. Yahweh, like Ahura Mazdāh, deserves to be king now but will rule as king *in some eschatological future*.[17] What contact was there between this congenial doctrine and the Jews in the Persian Empire?

Probably there was very little cultural exchange between Zoroaster or his followers and the prophets of Yahweh or their followers during Zoroaster's lifetime. Chorasmia was situated far from the center of Babylonian power and even farther from Palestine. It is likely that Zoroaster's influence spread only during the time when Persian kings were representing that influence to their empire in their own personal religion.

Vīshtāspa's conversion was the initial link between Zoroastrian tradition and the line of Persian kings. Subsequent to his conversion by Zoroaster, Vīshtāspa had his first son in 550 B.C. We know he had been converted because he gave the boy a Zoroastrian name which the Greeks simplified to Darius. Five years later Cyrus took eastern Iran, and Vīshtāspa exchanged his minor kingship for the more important post of satrap in the expanding Persian Empire. His son became spear bearer to Emperor Cambyses. Thus Darius, the son of a Zoroastrian family, was put in a position to claim kingship of the empire even though Vīshtāspa belonged to only a collateral branch of the Achaemenid family which had a claim to the Persian throne.

Darius went on to make the claim good by killing a certain Gaumata who had seized the throne from Cambyses, even though his father and grandfather were still alive and by rights should have preceded him to the throne. After the young boy had become king, he championed an element of Persian culture that would have recommended itself to the Jewish people's respect for law as the divinely appointed medium of order in history. Persian respect for truth and abhorrence of lies had long been legendary in Herodotus' time.[18] But the great lawgiver among the Persians was Darius. This is what Plato remembered him for and there is evidence that his law still carried weight toward the end of the third century—more than a hundred years after the breakup of the Persian Empire.[19]

After establishing the capital at Susa in 521 B.C., Darius turned immediately to the compilation and publication of a lawbook. It was modeled on the code of Hammurabi which accounts for its similarity to Jewish law. And, like that code, Darius also claimed that his god, Ahura Mazdāh, was the lawgiver. An inscription reads, "O man, what is the command of Ahura Mazdāh, let this not seem repugnant to you; do not depart from righteousness, do not revolt."[20] It is perhaps significant that Darius uses *dat* for his law which is the equivalent of the Hebrew *dath* found in Esther and Ezra.[21] There is evidence that Darius' lawbook was published almost immediately and that it quickly became obligatory throughout the empire.[22] Daniel and Esther reveal the atmosphere of awe and respect this law engendered among the Jews when they refer to Darius' code as "the law of the Medes and the Persians, which cannot be revoked" (Dan. 6:8, 12, 15; Esth. 1:19).

The point of the establishment of this congeniality of religious cultures is to posit the possibility of a contribution of Persian to Jewish religious thought. Such a possibility exists wherever a dominant culture is in chronological and geographical proximity to a subject culture. We have seen that Darius communicated his religious convictions throughout the empire in the very first years of his reign by means of his lawbook. This put Persian religious culture in the requisite chronological and geographical proximity to Jewish culture. But we must be more precise in our description of the religious culture the Persian kings represented. It was not the pure doctrine of Zoroaster.

Darius must have had direct contact with Zoroaster in the court of his father, Vīshtāspa, under whose shelter Zoroaster worked. But Darius was not a pure Zoroastrian, although he probably held the basic doctrines of Zoroaster.[23] He shows the influence of Zoroaster's monotheistic reform in his recognition of Ahura Mazdāh as the supreme Lord. But he does not deny the existence of other gods. Consequently he did not destroy any national cult which he found among the subject peoples of his empire.

Xerxes, Darius' son, also shows the influence of Zoroaster in his religious policy in the empire.[24] Like his father, he worshiped Ahura Mazdāh as the creator of heaven and earth, but he acknowledged other gods. His special connection with Zoroastrian tradition comes to the fore in a proclamation he issued forbidding the worship of daevas in the empire. We noted above that this had been Zoroaster's way of reforming the polytheistic tradition that came to him.

But our primary interest in Zoroastrian religious culture is not its monotheistic strain. Judaism certainly did not borrow that. We have mentioned that only to establish an important positive relationship between the two cultures. Our main concern has to do with another doctrine of Zoroaster that appears in Xerxes' daeva inscription. The conclusion of that inscription reads: "The man who has respect for the law which Ahura

Mazdāh has established and who worships Ahura Mazdāh in accordance with Trust and using the proper rite, may he be both happy when alive *and blessed when dead.*"[25] The last phrase is the pivotal one. Zoroaster believed in a life after death and Xerxes not only believed in it but depended upon it as the sanction to enforce the law of the empire. Judaism has left no record of such a belief in life after death in the Persian period. This inscription of Xerxes at Persepolis is the first documentation in the period under discussion when the dominant, friendly, and religiously congenial Persian culture offered the doctrine of another world to the subject Jewish culture. But we need to return to Zoroaster to appreciate the full connotation of Xerxes' offer to be "blessed when dead."

In Zoroaster's teaching, postmortem blessing for the individual was only one side of a more inclusive doctrine of another world. The other side had to do with the renewal and continuation of communal life worked out in terms of a kingdom. In Zoroaster's doctrine of God we have already seen that Ahura Mazdāh dwelt in a kingdom that would be purified of evil in the last days. In this purified kingdom there was no rejection of material existence as inferior to spiritual. The future kingdom was a place where material blessings abound and where the individual experienced these blessings in a body. Zoroaster embraced the material universe as warmly as the Israelite.

Zaehner traces a probable development in Zoroaster's thought from a stage when he expected to reform life on earth to a stage when it became necessary for him to posit another life and another world for the blessing which Ahura Mazdāh guaranteed.[26] In one of the earliest portions of the Zoroastrian sacred texts, called the *Gatha* of the Seven Chapters, probably composed not long after Zoroaster's death, there is a specific reference to two worlds. It occurs in a prayer to "attain to thy good kingdom, O Ahura Mazdāh, for ever and ever. May a good ruler, whether man or woman, rule over the two worlds, O most wise among existent beings."[27]

It will illumine Judaism's eventual adoption of this future world if we note the occasions that prompted Zoroastrians to develop the doctrine in the first place. Zoroaster originally had a vision of purity and righteousness for this world which would be realized by the powers which Ahura Mazdāh gave his devotees. This vision took the form of a kingdom free of the lies and darkness that oppose the spirit of truth and light. But Zoroaster came to see that this could not be accomplished within one world so he put the victory and blessing off to another world. The other world, therefore, first developed as a compensation for the frustrations of history. It provided a new opportunity to realize hopes that had been dashed by history. Zoroaster's followers experienced a comparable frustration when they lost their official standing as the religion of the ruling power. This happened when Cyrus became king and the court of Vīshtāspa ceased to have a privileged position. Now Zoroastrianism became merely one religion in a vast empire with a multiplicity of religious traditions. Just when Zoroastrianism lost its special status, Zaehner detects in the *Gatha* of the Seven Chapters the emergence of reliance on another world.

Through the medium of a friendly and religiously congenial Persian Empire we have seen how the idea of a future world was made available to Judaism. So we may reasonably expect that when the Jewish people met with a severe enough frustration of their own hopes for history, they would follow the lead of the impressive culture under which they prospered for two centuries.

To complete the story of Zoroastrianism's relation to the Persian Empire in the reign of Artaxerxes I, which began in 465 B.C., Zoroastrianism became the official religion of the Achaemenian kings. The name Artaxerxes, "kingdom of righteousness," shows that his father intended that he should rule the empire under the guidance of Zoroastrian doctrine. The decisive indication that Zoroastrianism became official under this king is the new calendar adopted about 441 B.C. This calendar named the months after the chief deities of popular Zoroastrianism.[28] Zoroastrianism continued to be the official religion through the reign of Darius III until the empire ended in defeat at the hands of Alexander the Great in 333 B.C. This official Zoroastrianism of the Achaemenian kings no longer championed the strict monotheism of the founding prophet, although a reforming community of his followers who retained monotheism probably always continued to have an influence in the empire.

Whatever the regressions of official Zoroastrianism to pre-Zoroaster polytheism, the Magi, the priests who administered the religion, always preserved the tradition of some other world where an all-powerful, righteous Lord would repair the disappointments of common life. When the Jews were under Persian hegemony the situation was pleasant enough not to need that option. But the time was coming when the Jews would suffer such blasting of their own hopes that they would be happy to follow the lead of their former masters.

With the coming of Alexander the Great, the cultural climate changed. If it was accurate to describe Persian culture as friendly and congenial and therefore relatively permissive, it would be equally accurate by contrast to describe Hellenistic culture as aggressive. Alexander's campaign was a crusade to bring civilized Greek culture to Orientals.[29] In the course of Alexander's campaign and during its aftermath, the Jews of Palestine were simply at the mercy of the ebb and flow of competing powers. The settled times were over. The persecution of Jews for adherence to their religion no doubt had the effect of destroying the illusion of the adequacy of the Chronicler's view of history as the sphere of rewards or punishments for obedience or disobedience of the law. The historical situation of the Jews was similar to the situation at the time of the collapse of the prophetic view and the available Jewish theories of history had no adequate explanation for the flood of world events that now engulfed them.

Alexander crossed the Hellespont in 334 B.C. Palestinian Syria, including Judea, submitted in 332 B.C. While preparing to open a maritime route from Babylon to Egypt around Arabia in 323 B.C. Alexander died, and, no provision having been made for a successor, his empire soon broke apart. It was not until 275 B.C. that the situation finally stabilized. At that time, three dynasties, descended from three of Alexander's generals, emerged: the Seleucids ruled most of what had been Persian Asia, now called Syria; the Ptolemies ruled Egypt; the Antigonids ruled Macedonia. A fourth European dynasty sponsored by Rome, the Attalids of Pergamum, gained influence in Asia Minor. In 212 B.C. Rome began to exercise what became a controlling interest in Hellenistic affairs. As events worked themselves out, Ptolemaic Egypt acquired Judea in 301 B.C. and held it until 200 B.C.

The first hundred years of Hellenistic rule were quiet enough not to precipitate the crisis toward which Jewish history was steadily moving. The movement to homogenize the cultures of what had been the Persian Empire under the banner of Greek civilization would soon reach its high point. Then the indigenous cultures would react against the cultural imperialism of the crusade Alexander had unleashed.

The ironic thing about the Jewish reaction was that Jews provoked it, not Hellenistic kings. Certain elements within Judaism were willing to be more aggressive about assimilating Judaism to Greek ways than any of their Hellenistic overlords.[30] This must have been felt as an especially aggravating factor in the collapse of history for the Jews.

The familiar story of this collapse builds toward its climax under Jason. He purchased the high priesthood from Antiochus Epiphanes, the king of Syria, by offering 140 talents in addition to the usual tribute of 300. Revolutionary political reform followed the appointment of Jason. For an additional 150 talents Jason received permission to convert Jerusalem into a Greek polis named Antioch in honor of its patron, Antiochus. This enabled Jason to build a gymnasium and ephebeum, which was the school system designed to prepare young men for citizenship in the polis. He also registered a portion of the people of Jerusalem as official citizens. The council of elders, which had been the ruling body before, probably became the boule of the new city.

Now the devotees of Hellas had the institutions by which they could enjoy the advantages of civilization in style. The gymnasium was built under the fortress on the Temple hill and young men, including priests, flocked to it. They wore distinctive hats that marked them as patrons of the gymnasium and of course exercised unclothed. Antioch of Jerusalem could now send envoys to the athletic games held every fifth year at Tyre.

The most revolutionary aspect of Jason's return was the change of constitution involved in becoming a city. Under the prior political arrangement Jews were permitted to live according to their ancestral laws, which included, of course, the conduct of life according to the Mosaic law.[31] The "ancestral laws" had served as the constitution. Jason made a substitution. As reported in I and II Maccabees. "He set aside the existing royal concessions to the Jews . . . ; and he destroyed the lawful ways of living and introduced new customs contrary to the law." (II Macc. 4:11.) "And some of the people eagerly went to the king. He authorized them to observe the ordinance of the Gentiles." (I Macc. 1:13.) This did not mean that those Jews who preferred to be observant were hindered from following the law of Moses. It did mean that it ceased to be part of the law of the land in Judea. A Hellenistic way of life was now provided for constitutionally. This was a fundamental change. Not since Ezra had any other way of life been legal for Jews in Jerusalem. Jason's reform was the undoing of Ezra's reform. This defeat of the Jewish way of life, asked for and arranged for by Jewish leaders, must have inspired horror in the eyes of traditional Jews. They would have had to wonder how the Lord of history could permit such a development.

Already before Jason's reform there was a loss of confidence in the Chronicler's interpretation of history as the arena where justice, under law, is done. The "gentle cynic" who wrote Ecclesiastes, perhaps in the third century B.C., had ceased to be able to believe the conventional wisdom about history in his time.[32] He reduced to absurdity the traditional view that the wise were rewarded appropriately by pointing out that life goes as badly for the wise as it does for the foolish. Only a residual confidence in the possibility of some modest enjoyment of life preserved him from despair. If we ask where the blame lay for this pessimism, surely it cannot be the author's. He believed in God. But he was being asked to believe in a theory of God's activity in history that could not be supported by the facts of experience. If the orthodox theory of history failed in normal times, it is not difficult to imagine the threat that the developments under Jason posed to that theory. The worst was not yet.

Jason had apparently been a compromise candidate for the Hellenizing faction. He was willing to be the instrument of opening the doors legally for a Hellenized way of life, but belonging as he did to the high-priestly family with its deeply ingrained respect for the Jewish way of life, perhaps he could not be induced to act in contempt of the law. The Hellenizers found such a Jew in Menelaus. Since the availability of the high priesthood to the highest bidder had been established when Jason took office, this precedent was now used against Jason. Menelaus took the office away from Jason by offering the king three hundred talents more than Jason had paid.

This must have come as a shock to all who respected Jewish tradition, for this high priest had no hereditary right to his office. Tcherikover conjectures that popular revolt broke out at this point. There is no evidence of it in the records, but Menelaus soon provided the stimulus for revolt that was recorded.

Menelaus had bid more for his post than he was able to pay at the time. When pressed for the money he went to Antioch to placate the king. Antiochus was not in residence, but Menelaus won over the king's deputy by a present of several gold vessels confiscated from the Temple. This disregard for the sanctity of the Temple produced two immediate reactions. A former high priest, residing in Antioch, and learning of the gift, issued a public rebuke there. In Jerusalem, Menelaus' brother and deputy, Lysimachus, who had removed the vessels from the Temple for his brother, had to face popular unrest at his sacrilege. The author of II Maccabees used one of the worst epithets available in the Hellenistic world when he called Lysimachus a "temple robber" (II Macc. 4:42). Before the populace could act, Lysimachus armed about three thousand men and attacked the people of Jerusalem. In the riot that ensued, the crowds overwhelmed the soldiers and killed Lysimachus.

The Jews appealed to the king against the sacrilege of Menelaus but to no avail. The three Jerusalem envoys who carried the protest to Antiochus were put to death. The frustration of this appeal to the final court of justice left the Jews no recourse but revolt. Curiously enough, Jason, the ex-high priest, was the leader of the first organized assault.

Antiochus himself exacerbated the situation by appropriating Temple funds upon his return from a campaign in Egypt in 169 B.C. From Antiochus' point of view this may have been justified by his financial needs, but the removal of the furniture of the Temple used in connection with the cult could only strike Jews as an outrageous act directed against their deepest religious convictions. Under the circumstances it is surprising that the first armed attack on Jerusalem did not come then. A rumor that Antiochus had been killed on a second campaign against Egypt brought it on. Jason gathered a force of about a thousand men and attacked Jerusalem from Transjordan. He controlled the city for a time, forcing Menelaus into the citadel, but his senseless killing of his fellow Jews produced a popular reaction and he withdrew.

This was enough to convince Antiochus that Jerusalem was out of control. He came personally to put down the revolt. His soldiers killed thousands of inhabitants and sold thousands into slavery.

As part of the punishment and securing of the city, Jerusalem was settled with aliens—Syrian soldiers who brought their own religious rites with them. With typical Hellenistic readiness to equate the god of one nation with the god of another, the Syrian soldiers probably commandeered the Jerusalem Temple for their own worship. This would account for the prostitution in the Temple—a horror to Jews and a perfectly natural adjunct to worship for Syrians.[33]

The final outrage of Antiochus was the outlawing of the Jewish way of life. (II Macc. 6:1 ff.) Under Jason the non-Jewish, Hellenistic way of life had become constitutional. Now it became obligatory. Circumcision was prohibited upon pain of death as was the observance of Sabbaths and annual feasts. Even confession of adherence to the Jewish religion was denied to Jews. They were forced to participate in pagan festivals. The culmination was the erection in the Temple of the famous "abomination of desolation" mentioned in Dan. 11:31; I Macc. 1:54; and Mark 13:14. It was probably an idol or stone appropriate to the Syrian cult which, however, II Macc. 6:2 calls Zeus Olympus. Judaism was outlawed even in the Greek cities around Judea.

How could religious persecution such as this get started in a culture that was noted for its religious tolerance? We can assume that events in Judea must have convinced Antiochus that the religion of the Jews was the source of, or at least an important stimulus to, political unrest. Most probably he concluded that this people could only become loyal subjects if they were denied their strange seditious religion. Although Antiochus' interest in the matter was strictly political, this persecution touched Judaism at a much deeper level. It called for a revolution in religious outlook.

The problem for Judaism was: How could the God of history permit something like the persecution of Antiochus to happen? The prophets had promised the Jews some saving act comparable to the exodus. Instead, God's people were being destroyed. The Chronicler had promised blessing in return for obedience, instead true religion was being punished. The perse-

cution fell precisely upon the faithful. History rewarded faithfulness with death. Attempts to preserve the Jewish religion
ended in defilement of its Temple and the destruction of all its
public institutions. The crisis this involved for Jewish belief
cannot be exaggerated. Jews had been distinguished by their
belief in a God who was the Lord of history. Now history had
failed them. Could they continue to believe in their God and
the value of history that he represented? They could if some-
where history's frustrated promises might still be fulfilled. Such
a place had been available in Israel's cultural heritage since
Cyrus.

Credit goes to the author of The Book of Daniel for bringing
to life this other place for Judaism. This other place was a future world where the faithful individual would rise from death
to a new life, and where God's will would be the rule for a new
worldwide order called the Kingdom of God. It is perhaps in-
dicative of the Persian influence that some of Daniel's stories
took place in the reigns of the Persian kings, Cyrus and Darius.
Of course the idea of life after death was current in Hellenistic
culture, but their conception did not include either the body or
history, as did the life after death as it had been conceived in
Persian culture. And since the Palestinian Jewish community
was suffering at the hands of Hellenistic culture, it is unlikely
that it would choose this culture as its source for the other
world anyway. The process we have been describing in this
chapter seems the more likely explanation of this tremendous
step into a future world: Persian culture had made the idea of
another world available in a friendly and congenial setting.
Once Israel had exhausted the possibilities of history in some
way similar to Zoroaster's experience of the frustration of his
hopes, it became ready for this new leap of faith.

The leap into the future world of personal and communal fulfillment was *not* a simple leap away from history. It would be
too cynical to describe what Daniel found as merely a way to
escape history. In fact, the opposite was more the case. The future world made it possible for Judaism to continue to stay

with history by offering a new vantage point from which a more adequate understanding of history could unfold.[34]

The persecution of Antiochus proved that the prophetic view of history and the Chronicler's view of history both took inadequate account of the God-contrary and chaotic forces in history. Judaism had been too optimistic about history and too trusting in what even omnipotence could accomplish. The future world freed Judaism for a more realistic reading of history and renewed its courage to participate in its affairs. The resultant view of history is usually called apocalyptic.

The apocalyptic reading of history was the recovery of the prophetic vision of history with the inclusion of a future world for God's decisive saving action. It also included a larger canvas upon which to paint the history of this world, with room for the roles of the powerful nations and their failure to serve God's plan. There was even scope for a mythical head of the opposition.

It is curious how many Christian scholars are embarrassed by the development of apocalyptic thought. They prefer to see the crown of Israel's reflection on history in the prophets. Martin Noth attempts to discredit the Daniel scheme of the successive world powers, culminating in the collapse that heralded the end of this world and the beginning of God's kingdom. Noth maintains that Daniel's scheme was not a serious reading of history since it pointed finally to a brief and calculated interval after which the future world would replace the present evil world.[35] One can only ask what other viable reading of history was possible for Judaism under the pressure of Antiochus' persecution and with a theological heritage that featured a powerful and just God of history. Given the depths of godlessness to which history had sunk, if Yahweh were just and powerful, believers had to expect him to do something soon. It is important to realize how complete the failure of history must have been for the victims of Antiochus' persecution. There could be no point in continuing a simple faith in history. Its possibilities had been exhausted.

The apocalyptic view of history was an extension of the prophetic view of history adjusted in the light of the Antiochus experience. Here too we find that Christian scholars are embarrassed with the apocalyptic solution and wish to dissociate it from the prophets.[36] Gerhard von Rad's main objection is that this literature neglects a prophetic recitation of Israel's saving history for a concentration upon the last generation of Israel.[37] But surely this misses the point of the experience under Antiochus. This experience persuaded Judaism that history offered no further possibility of a redemption in history like the exodus. This is what I mean by what I have called the collapse of the prophetic view. Only a view that could explain the demise of history was of any use at all. This was the contribution of Daniel and his later imitators. They were courageous and imaginative enough to absorb the worst that history could do to them and still make provision for the triumph of God and the salvation of his people.

Professor Muilenburg is fairer to apocalyptic than either Noth or von Rad. "Apocalptic actually represents a deepening of Israel's prophetic consciousness in the light of the destruction of the nation and the somber years of suffering and tragedy which followed."[38]

Daniel's solution to history became the standard one for Judaism. His vision of the future world with its everlasting life for the righteous individual and an everlasting kingdom of peace and justice for the people of God was repeated with variations by the whole class of literature called apocalyptic which stretched from Daniel, written sometime between 167 and 163 B.C., to the book of Revelation, written toward the end of the first century A.D.[39] This expectation of the next world became one of the distinctive doctrines of the most influential party in Judaism. The Pharisees came to prominence in the Maccabean period when the doctrine of a future life was the supportive companion to their main doctrine of obedience to the Law at all costs. No doubt a large part of their success in winning popular support was due to their adoption of the future world which

their political adversaries, the Sadducees, were unwilling to accept.[40] The other great party in Judaism, the Essenes, shared
the doctrine of the future world with the Pharisees. This is well
documented in the literature of the Qumran community which
drew from Daniel and other apocalyptics, and also created
some of its own. And finally, the Jewish sect that followed Jesus
of Nazareth eventually gave a Platonic form to the future world
and it became part of the heritage of Western civilization.

How are we to evaluate this step into another world? First,
we must insist that it happened naturally enough. Until the
crisis that culminated in the repressive measures of Antiochus
Epiphanes, the Jewish people had a grand but incomplete theology of history. They assumed that history was directed by the
irresistible power of the same just and saving God who had
brought Israel out of Egypt. It was incomplete as a theory because it did not take adequate account of the ability of the
world in which they lived to resist the just and saving purposes
even of the God of the exodus. But under the Persians the Jewish people were exposed to a more complete theology—one that
took the recalcitrance of history fully into account without giving way to despair. This theory of history was worked out by
Zoroaster in terms of a dualism that explained the recalcitrance
by attributing it to an evil mythical opponent of the supreme
God. Then, resultant conflict was resolved by the evolution of
a future world where efforts in behalf of the supreme God
would be rewarded by life after death and dualistic history
would be replaced by an everlasting kingdom of good.

It was natural for Judaism to adopt this Persian solution as its
own once the resistance of history to the purposes of God became strong enough. What made the Persian solution even
more natural was its own parallels to Jewish monotheism.

Until now I have avoided one aspect of the question of Jewish dependence upon Persian culture for its doctrine of another
world; namely, its relation to a theory of revelation. In the theological opinion of some, the people of God can never learn
anything substantial from another culture. Their only source of

doctrine must be direct communication from God and these doctrines so revealed must be distinguished by being quite unique compared to similar doctrines in other cultures. I do not share that theory of revelation. My assumption is that the experiences the Jewish religious community had in common with its surrounding culture formed the basis of many of its own doctrines. Further, when the surrounding culture had formulated some conviction about the nature of reality on the basis of a more mature experience than the Jewish religious community possessed, that community was wise to enlarge the scope of its "revelation" to include such a formulation.[41]

The step into the other world was a natural one. It was also a wise one. It was wise because, given the world of the time, there was no feasible way to preserve the values for human life in a history enshrined in Jewish religion without banking them in the safety of another world. The other world was a safe bank because it was not open to moth and rust and thievery—the corroding effects of unfortunate historical experience.

Historical experience was almost bound to be unfortunate for the vast majority of people who lived in Hellenistic times. The Hellenistic world was not open to much improvement from within. Slave labor was the basis of civilized accomplishment and would continue until some substitute came along to make it dispensable. The economic organization was a kind of laissez-faire capitalism with little protection for the poor and indebted. Its effect was to confine affluence to an ever-smaller number of wealthy men while it tended to strip the poor of what means they had. The theory of Hellenistic kingship made the political system unresponsive to the needs of the common man. International relations were so unstable that constant wars robbed most men of even the modest security and economic and political arrangements permitted. With such instability and want, it is no wonder that the Kingdom of God often came to be envisioned as a peaceful feast. Far from being merely a flight from the world in which they lived, the next world of the Jews in mid-second century B.C. made it possible for them to continue to live humanely. It will, I think, be no exaggeration to say that until recently the Western world has only remained as civilized as it has because it has lived off the interest deposited in the future world. But whether this happy influence upon history can maintain itself now is the question that prompts my third evaluation.

The Danielic step into another world was so timely that it was also probably temporary. Any step that was so in tune with its particular times, so much a product of its own times, will probably need to be replaced with choreography more apt for our times. Our times are fundamentally different from Hellenistic times in that now there are the technological means and political theories that make possible a long, affluent, and highly civilized life on earth for most of its inhabitants. By technological means, I refer to birth control, scientific agriculture, the automated production of goods and services, together with modern scientific medical care. By political theories, I refer to those which aim at a political process that enlists the involvement of all those affected by political decisions. By highly civilized life, I mean the possibility of exploring meaning and fulfillment in life free from material needs, physical needs, and organized threats to individuals and communities. Given that the world around us now does offer these new possibilities for life, it must be reevaluated. Perhaps now there is a real prospect of achieving on earth what the Jews in the Hellenistic age could only hope for in heaven.

An equally weighty argument for phasing out the next world is the growing, spreading conviction in our time that there is little credible evidence that it exists. This is not just a matter of religious conviction. Dreams, visions, appearances, heavenly messengers ascending and descending, simply do not count now in the way they did in the Hellenistic age. Therefore large numbers of men have very little reason now, compared to then, to need a second world, let alone bank our most precious values in it.

I hope now that our declared project, to devise a form of

Christianity without another world, does not seem so unnatural as it may have before we review the story of that world's dawning. If our fathers in the second century B.C. had the opportunity to usher in an extra world, their sons in the twentieth century A.D. should have the opportunity to usher it out. That generation lived to see it rise. This generation may live to see it set.

If the next world were to be phased out in our time, it would have momentous ramifications. But this happening need not destroy or impoverish true religion. Any decision against the future world should be with the same intention that prompted Daniel, namely, to preserve, enrich, and implement the redeeming purpose of God for his people as this has been declared all along in the tradition. The step back from another world should be as logical for respecters of tradition now as the step into it was for traditionalists then.

Just as naturally, there will be dissent from the new step we are exploring now—as there was then. The Sadducees refused to step into another world because tradition up until that time did not prescribe it and their experience of history did not dispose them to want it. They were certainly correct about the tradition. They were equally correct about their own experience of history. The Sadducees belonged largely to the rising *bourgeoisie* class of the Hellenistic age who shared whatever achievements of civilization and political power their age made available in the cities. For such people, also among the Jews, this world still offered means of providing for their own wellbeing. Their experience of history was not so frustrating as their poorer, less powerful, compatriots, whose religion brought them into collision with Hellenistic ways.

There are those today who will point out that tradition does not prescribe withdrawal from the other world. They will certainly be correct. They will also appeal to their experience of frustration in history, which cannot be denied them. Room must be allowed for this dissent. The conversation it provokes should be illuminating. For example, the this-worldly man might ask the otherworldly man if he has taken adequate account of the new means available to advance mankind's well-being. The otherworldly man might ask the this-worldly man if he has not noticed the unprecedented tragedy these new means make possible. The discussion is already well under way. This book wishes to be part of it.

But insofar as the conversation involves Christians, it assumes a special complication. When Judaism added its doctrine of the other world, massive as this addition was, no special saving act of God accompanied it to stamp it with special divine authority. This leaves the Jew freer to discuss the doctrine because to question it is not tantamount to questioning something like the exodus. For Christians the doctrine of another world is complicated by its connection with the resurrection of Christ. This is the definitive saving act of God for Christian tradition. It is often taken as the basis for belief in the other world to which Christ rose and to which Christians are to rise. To deny the other world seems to involve denial of the resurrection. This is taken to mean the denial of Christianity, of Christ. To this supposed complication we now turn to see that it is neither so necessary nor so complicated as it may seem.

NOTES

1. Written in the last quarter of the second century B.C.

2. Possibly from the second half of the fourth century B.C.

3. Otto Eissfeldt, *The Old Testament: An Introduction* (Harper & Row, Publishers, Inc., 1965), p. 442.

4. For what follows, see mainly Gerhard von Rad, *Old Testament Theology: The Theology of Israel's Prophet Traditions* (Harper & Row, Publishers, Inc., 1965), Vol. II, pp. 238–300.

5. Albert Olmstead, *History of the Persian Empire* (The University of Chicago Press, 1948), p. 57.

6. Deutero-Isaiah comes between 550 and 538 B.C. (Eissfeldt, *op. cit.*, p. 337); Trito-Isaiah, in the last third of the sixth century B.C. (*ibid.*, p. 349).

7. Olmstead, *op. cit.*, p. 113.

8. *Ibid.*, p. 138.

9. *Ibid.*, pp. 141–142.

10. Elias J. Bickerman places him in the first half of the fourth century ("The Historical Foundations of Postbiblical Judaism," in *The Jews: Their History, Culture, and Religion*, ed. by Louis Finkelstein, 1st ed., Vol. I, p. 81; Harper & Brothers, 1949). Eissfeldt prefers the middle or last half of that century (*op. cit.*, p. 540).

11. Bickerman, *op. cit.*, p. 81, and for the above interpretation of the Chronicler, see pp. 77–82.

12. *Ibid.*, p. 269.

13. This translation of the Cyrus cylinder is from James B. Pritchard, *The Ancient Near East: An Anthology of Texts and Pictures* (Pinceton University Press, 1958), 9.207.

14. William Foxwell Albright, "The Biblical Period," in Bickerman, *op. cit.*, p. 53, referring to the judgments of Eduard Meyer and Hans Heinrich Schaeder.

15. For this interpretation of the agreement, see Bickerman, *op. cit.*, p. 95.

16. R. C. Zaehner, *The Dawn and Twilight of Zoroastrianism* (G. P. Putnam's Sons, 1961), p. 33; Olmstead, *op cit.*, p. 94.

17. Zaehner, *op. cit.*, p. 60.

18. "They hold it unlawful to talk of anything which it is unlawful to do. The most disgraceful thing in the world, they think, is to tell a lie." (Herodotus I. 139.)

19. Olmstead, *op. cit.*, p. 130.

20. Quoted in *ibid.*, p. 123, from Nagsh-i-Rustam A6.

21. Esth. 1:8, 12–15, and elsewhere; Ezra 7:26, where the law of Yahweh and the law of king Artaxerxes are both declared obligatory for the Jews.

22. Olmstead, *op. cit.*, p. 119, where he cites a text that refers to the lawbook in Babylonia in 519.

23. Cf. Zaehner, *op. cit.*, on "The Zoroastrianism of Darius," pp. 156–160.

24. For a description of Xerxes' Zoroastrianism, see Zaehner, *op. cit.*, pp. 159–160.

25. Cited in Zaehner, *op. cit.*, p. 159. Cf. Olmstead, *op. cit.*, p. 232.

26. Zaehner, *op. cit.*, pp. 58–59.

27. *Ibid.*, pp. 73, 74.

28. *Ibid.*, p. 155.

29. The crusade was advocated as far back as 370 by Isocrates, who desired that all Greeks should unite to attack Persia. (W. W. Tarn, *Hellenistic Civilization*, 3d ed., rev. by Tarn and G. T. Griffith, p. 80; The World Publishing Company, 1952.)

30. The account given follows the reconstruction of events of Victor Tcherikover, *Hellenistic Civilization and the Jews*, tr. by S. Applebaum (The Jewish Publication Society of America, 1961).

31. Josephus, *Antiquities*, xii. 138 ff.

32. Eissfeldt, *op. cit.*, p. 495.

33. Bickerman isolated the Syrian character of the cult instituted at the time of Antioch's persecution. Tcherikover explains this cult as the native religion the new Syrian element brought with them into Jerusalem.

34. The Maccabean activity proves Judaism's continued interest in history.

35. Martin Noth, *Das Geschichtsverständnis der alttestamentlichen Apokalyptik*, Arbeitsgemeinschaft für Forschung des Landes Nordrhein-Westfalen, Heft 21 (Köln: Westdeutscher Verlag, 1953).

36. Cf. von Rad's opinion: "It might seem appropriate to understand apocalyptic literature as a child of prophecy. To my mind, however, this is completely out of the question." (*Old Testament Theology*, Vol. II, p. 303.)

37. *Ibid.*, p. 304.

38. James Muilenburg, in *The Interpreter's Bible* (Abingdon Press, 1952), Vol. 1, p. 340. Cf. R. H. Charles: "Prophecy and Apocalyptic are not opposed to each other, essentially; for

fundamentally they have a common basis, they use for the most part the same methods, and are both alike radically ethical." (*Eschatology*, p. 173; Schocken Books, Inc., 1913.) H. H. Rowley, in *The Relevance of Apocalyptic* (3d ed., Association Press, 1963), shares this opinion.

39. Eissfeldt, *op. cit.*, pp. 520–521. Cf. Rowley, *op. cit.*, for a brief survey of the other world in each apocalyptic work.

40. Louis Finkelstein, *The Pharisees* (The Jewish Publication Society of America, 1962), Vol. I, p. 157.

41. There is a vast and inconclusive literature on the relation of Persian religion to Jewish doctrine. Mostly it reflects the theory of revelation each author assumes but seldom states. The possibility of Judaism's borrowing from Persian religious tradition in the second century B.C. is established even for those most opposed to such borrowing by the case of the obviously Persian doctrine of the two spirits which appears in the Qumran Manual of Discipline, III.13 to IV.26. Cf. Bo Reicke: "Hier könnte eine direkte Übernahme iranischer Traditionen vorliegen" ("Iranische Religion, Judentum und Urchristentum," *Die Religion in Geschichte und Gegenwart*, Vol. III, col. 283, where also the literature is given). In the midst of a section that rejects the influence of pagan myth on Israel's hope of salvation because of the widely differing views of history, Walther Eichrodt must admit, if only in a footnote: "Eine Ausnahme bildet nur die Zarathustra-Religion; sie ist charakteristischerweise wie die mosäische Religion eine Stifterreligion, die im Gegensatz zu den alten Kultreligionen steht. Ihr Einfluss auf die spätjüdische Religion, der oben berührt wurde, ist im einzelnen schwer festzustellen" (*Theologie des Alten Testaments*, Teil I, p. 338, n. 124). A. von Gall, in *Basileia tou Theou* (Heidelberg: Winters Universitätsbuchhandlung, 1926), makes the most detailed case for Jewish use of Persian eschatology. For literature on Zoroastrianism, cf. Zaehner, *op. cit.*, pp. 339–348.

II

THE RESURRECTION OF JESUS, THE COMPOSITION OF THE GOSPELS, AND THE WORLD TO COME

Paul and the Earliest Church

In order to be able to define the relation between the other world that dawned under the Maccabees and the resurrection of Jesus, we must examine the New Testament records, first to see precisely how that resurrection was experienced and then how it stimulated the composition of the Gospels which provide us with official interpretations of Jesus in the church.

Whatever impression Jesus made upon those he met, it was forty to one hundred years before the community that eventually worshiped him deemed these impressions worth gathering into the connected accounts we call our Gospels.[1] According to our records, the role of Jesus' life within the life of the church was negligible for almost forty years.

Paul is our chief witness to this period.[2] It is striking how seldom he made any use of material from Jesus' life. Paul knew that the church traced Jesus' lineage to David (Rom. 1:3). Apart from the crucifixion, Paul apparently had knowledge of only one other incident in Jesus' career—he recounted the last supper with the disciples on the night of his betrayal (I Cor. 11:23-25). And even this information he claimed to have gotten not from current church tradition but directly from the risen Lord ("I received from the Lord . . . ," v. 23).

There are only three cases where Paul seemed to use a particular tradition of the teaching of Jesus. Once he assured the faltering Thessalonians by "the word of the Lord," that, at Christ's return, dead Christians would be raised and translated to heaven ahead of surviving Christians (I Thess. 4:15). On another occasion he based his own position against divorce upon a charge of the Lord (I Cor. 7:10). Presumably he was following a tradition of Jesus' teaching. Finally, Paul justified financial support of the preachers in the church by a command of the Lord (I Cor. 9:14).

That is all the use Paul makes of Jesus. And in one of these cases he went out of his way to distinguish his source as the risen Lord in distinction from the church's tradition about Jesus. Claims have been made that there was much more of Jesus' teaching in Paul than Paul would admit. These claims are based on parallels between Paul's ethical exhortations and sayings of Jesus. Such parallels are surely no proof of more than the fact that Jesus and Paul belonged to some extent to a common heritage of Jewish ethical instruction.

If Jesus' ministry was available to the church Paul represents, it would seem that Paul was avoiding it on principle, which may be the point of II Cor. 5:16. This is the usual way of explaining the absence of Jesus in Paul's writings. The supposition is that abundant material about Jesus' teaching and activity was current in Paul's church but Paul avoided using it to protect his apostolic office from dependence upon the other apostles who had been companions of Jesus (Gal., chs. 1; 2).

I am not convinced. Material about Jesus ministry is just as scarce in the non-Pauline letters. Moreover, if words and actions of Jesus had been available to settle the disputes in which Paul was almost continuously embroiled, it is difficult to imagine how such material could have been so consistently and successfully suppressed. When Paul appealed to Jesus in argument, it was always, with the few exceptions noted, to the risen glorified Lord who communicated his will directly to Paul. This risen Jesus and not the Jesus of the earthly ministry must, I conclude, have been *the* canon for churchly conversation in Pauline circles.

But suppose for the sake of argument that the lack of Jesus-tradition in Paul was the result of his bias against it. Suppose the church of Paul was full of such tradition and that it was so well known to everyone that it required no mention. If these suppositions are true, it follows that the church of Paul must not have valued this Jesus tradition highly or considered it essential. For Paul's claim to apostolic authority in the church was based solely on contact with the risen Lord apart from any knowledge of Jesus' earthly life except that he lived and was crucified. The church accepted Paul as an apostle. In accepting him as an apostle, it accepted his evaluation of Jesus' earthly life. By implication, the church that recognized Paul by that act declared the knowledge of Jesus' ministry to have been peripheral and accidental to its gospel.

Even after our Gospels were composed, they did not immediately establish themselves as authoritative. The whole Jesus-tradition remained in flux until the middle of the second century. Prof. Helmut Köster has shown that, prior to Justin, the apostolic fathers were quite independent of our written Gospels.[3] When they had occasion to allude to Jesus' ministry, it was to the same floating, amorphous tradition that each Gospel author pressed into his own mold. Even after authors of the second-century church accustomed themselves to citing our written Gospels as canon, they still molded words of Jesus to suit their needs.[4]

It appears that the earliest church got along well enough for an extended period without a life of Jesus. If we can discover what suddenly triggered the composition of Mark and shaped it and the other Gospels, we shall be in a position to evaluate the way the church of the New Testament came to its interpretation of Jesus of Nazareth.

There are various ways of approaching what motivated Mark, Matthew, and Luke to write. I have chosen the witness to the resurrection of Jesus as the most fruitful starting point for understanding the composition of the Gospels. If this choice seems arbitrary, I hope it will vindicate itself in the course of the investigation. But even before we know how and where it might lead, resurrection witness does seem a likely starting point. There could hardly be a conviction more fundamental to the early church than its conviction that God had raised Jesus to life after his death. As we have seen, Paul's faith centered upon the risen Lord. In this he was typical of the whole church. One very good reflection of the faith of the whole church may be found in the short confessions that large segments of the church used. One such confession is cited in Rom. 1:3–4. According to this confessional statement the resurrection was the source of the church's conviction that Jesus was the Son of God. For in this resurrection his divine Sonship first came to light ("designated Son of God . . . by his resurrection from the dead"). Philippians 2:5-11 connects the conclusion, "Jesus Christ is Lord," to the center of the action in the hymn ("Therefore God has highly exalted him"). Jesus' resurrection took an equally central place in confessions found in I Peter 3-18; I Tim. 3:16; and Col. 1:15 f.

The primacy of resurrection over ministry in the faith of the early church is borne out in the records we have of the experience of the disciples. The writers of Matthew, Mark, and Luke were careful to limit whatever tentative appreciation of Jesus his followers may have had before his resurrection. As spokesman and leader of the disciples, Peter illustrates this best. In Matthew's story of Jesus walking on the water, only Peter had faith enough to ask to walk too. So far so good until his doubt sinks him and he receives the rebuke, "O man of little faith" (Matt. 14:31). Peter recognized Jesus' Messiahship at Caesarea Philippi but could not accept that this included crucifixion. So again, his defective faith earned a rebuke, "Get behind me, Satan!" (Mark 8:33). The same pattern unfolded on the Mount of Transfiguration. Peter honored the transfigured Jesus along with Moses and Elijah, but his failure to appreciate the superiority of Jesus had to be corrected by a voice from heaven (ch. 9:2 ff.). The limitation of Peter's insight was matched finally by failure to perform faithfully. Peter promised to be loyal in the face of Jesus' death (ch. 14:29). Still when the shepherd was struck down, the sheep fled as Jesus had predicted (v. 27). Peter capped the flight by his own denial of Jesus outside in the courtyard while Jesus was being examined inside. But then the resurrection occurred and the doubt and disloyalty of Peter and all the disciples was repaired. So far as we know they became distinguished apostles and martyrs.

Given this central role of resurrection to faith, it is surprising that it has not had more effect upon our understanding of the Gospels. Agreeing that all of Jesus' ministry is viewed from a resurrection perspective, it has been customary ever since Martin Kähler and early form criticism to account for our Gospels by reference to the passion narratives rather than to the resurrection stories.[5] It would certainly be more in keeping with the confessional posture of the church in the earliest records we have to give priority to the hypothesis that the Gospels are extended resurrection stories instead of the usual hypothesis that they are extended passion narratives.

When form criticism began to see that the tradition about Jesus circulated in isolated fragments before it was edited into some connected narrative by our Gospel writers, the question arose: What first prompted putting the fragments together? The initial answer is that the church needed to explain the crucifixion. Martin Dibelius, the famous Heidelberg professor of New Testament, typified this solution when he conjectured that the church was struck with embarrassment at believing a condemned and executed criminal was its Messiah. Consequently, it was forced immediately to develop an account of the crucifixion that explained the incongruity. This account was called the passion narrative. Then, the argument proceeded, the story of the rest of Jesus' career was added as prelude. This theory of the origin of the Gospels gave rise to the description of the Gospels as "extended passion narratives." I wish to challenge this theory of the origin of Gospel composition. It fails to explain why the Gospels were not composed until forty years or more after the church began to reflect on the crucifixion. In place of "extended passion narratives" I should like to propose that the Gospels are more accurately described as "extended resurrection stories." If we follow the story of the church's doctrine of the resurrection of Jesus, we shall discover that embarrassment over *resurrection* was what triggered the writing of the Gospels and not embarrassment over crucifixion.

When we scan the earliest materials outside the Gospels that witness to the resurrection, we discover that very little was said about the beginning of faith in the resurrection and what induced the conviction that Jesus had been raised. Information about the resurrection was not supplied; it was simply assumed and made the basis for other articles of faith. In fact only one passage deals directly with the resurrection and gives promise of revealing how the early church viewed it. That passage is I Cor., ch. 15.

Paul wrote I Cor., ch. 15, probably in A.D. 55 or 56,[6] but the chapter contains earlier material. It is, in effect, a commentary on a primitive confessional statement at the beginning of the chapter, in vs. 3–5:

> For I delivered to you as of first importance what I also received,
> that Christ died for our sins in accordance with the scriptures, that he was buried,
> that he was raised on the third day in accordance with the scriptures and
> that he appeared to Cephas, then to the twelve.

Several things about this statement alert us to its character and antiquity. The first line shows that the next four lines are tradition. The words "receive" and "deliver" correspond to the technical terms, *qibbel* and *nasar*, which describe the passing on of tradition in Judaism. This admission by Paul that he is using tradition is very exceptional. It is the only time in all his writings that Paul admitted dependence upon church tradition. His more typical use of those technical terms is exemplified in I Cor. 11:23, where the subject is the Lord's Supper tradition. Here Paul was not willing to admit that this was common churchly tradition. Instead he claimed it was private property revealed directly to him by the risen Lord ("For I received from the *Lord* what I also delivered to you"). "From the Lord" is omitted in ch. 15:3. This omission is Paul's way of claiming he would deal with the question of resurrection the way the church at large understood it and not merely as a piece of Pauline theology. The same claim was reiterated in v. 11: "Whether then it was I or they, so we preach and so you believed." Paul considered the problem the Corinthians were having so serious that he brought a churchly answer to bear. Thus this first line provides precisely what our investigation needs— a window upon the church's understanding of the resurrection of Jesus prior to the composition of the Gospels.

The style of the four lines that follow confirm what the introduction promised. Each line begins with the same Greek word for "that," showing that together they made up a fixed confessional formula.

The traditional character of the passage is further confirmed by the non-Pauline words and phrases it contains.[7] The phrase "for our sins" was not Paul's way of speaking of sin; that is to say, the six uses of the word for "sin" in the plural, with the genitive case or with an article, all of which occur together here, were not typical of Paul but reflect the influence of early Christian usage. In the fifty-six cases where Paul used the word himself *not* as a quotation, it was usually in the singular and never with a genitive. "In accordance with the scriptures" is found nowhere else in Paul. The word for "appeared" occurs only here in genuine Pauline letters. The word for "he was raised" is found only in this chapter. "The twelve" is unique to this passage. All these exceptional uses of language show that Paul did not write this confession. Indeed the style is not even from the same language Paul wrote. Joachim Jeremias finds four stylistic features that suggest Aramaic rather than Greek origin. This plus the double reference to the Old Testament makes plausible an original Palestinian Jewish context, for Palestinian Jews naturally used their native language, Aramaic, for their confessional statements and depended heavily on their Bible, the Old Testament.

It is interesting to speculate when this piece of tradition may have come to Paul. If the confession is early Jewish Christian, then it would be most at home in Jerusalem. Paul admitted two visits to Jerusalem early in his career—one three years after his conversion and another fourteen years afterward (Gal. 1:18; 2:1). On the first visit he saw only Peter and James, the two individuals whom Paul's tradition credits with private appearances (I Cor. 15:5, 7). James was not included in the confessional formula, but he was included in the six appearances Paul considered official for the church's belief in the resurrection of Jesus. This means it is probable that these appearances were already the officially recognized testimony to the resurrection in the thirties! Here then might be the starting point of primitive resurrection faith. After examining this starting point, we shall be in a position to make comparisons between resurrection appearance stories in the Gospels and the earliest record of appearances and to detect whether or not the church felt forced to make modifications to its basic conviction with the passage of time.

It is not necessary to attempt to explain each word and phrase of this earliest resurrection confession. However, certain elements are important for our investigations. The first and third lines of the last four show that the church explained Jesus' death and resurrection as the fulfillment of a predetermined plan of God revealed in the Old Testament. This attempt to explain these surprising events from Scripture probably explains the period of time between the death and resurrection—"on the third day."[8] This phrase most likely was taken from Hos. 6:2. It also may mean merely a period of indeterminate duration. The most important inference from "on the third day" relates to the second line of the confession—"he was buried." The point is that the church was convinced that Jesus was actually dead and that his resurrection was nothing less than a "resurrection from the dead."

In connection with this burial, it is important to note that there was no suggestion that an empty tomb was the first indication of resurrection. The initial indication of Jesus' resurrection according to this earliest witness was the appearance to Peter "and that he appeared to Cephas," which was then confirmed by an appearance to the Twelve. This primacy of Peter's witness and of the witness of the Twelve will provide a fair test of the age of other resurrection appearance accounts.

What happened in these "appearances"? What "was seen" by Peter and the Twelve? The Greek word here for "appeared," or "was seen," gives some indication of the kind of phenomenon the confession intended to describe.[9] The Greek word, especially with the dative for Cephas, emphasized the activity of the risen Jesus, who showed himself to the witness or was shown alive to them by God. That is a privilege of revelation experience and not the simple observation available to anyone who wishes to take notice of an object. All resurrection witnesses were believers. At the same time the witness really saw something. He was not dreaming and projecting his faith experience into visual form. Paul emphasized this in I Cor. 9:1, by using the active form of the verb *to see* not the passive, which is the usual form for revelations: "Have I not seen Jesus our Lord?"

Two things tend to encumber our understanding of the "seeing" in this confession. The first is the tendency of those who know the Gospel accounts of the appearances to read the Jesus of those appearances into I Cor., ch. 15. The Jesus of this earliest confession must not be presumed to be simply modeled after the earthly Jesus whom one could touch and to whom a meal might be served. The presumption is that Jesus was revealed or made his appearance *from heaven*. Paul was not met on the road to Damascus by one more traveler. Rather, the revelation came to him from heaven, as the light and voice from Luke's account indicates (Acts 9:3 ff.). Hans Grass gathers together all the revelational experiences in the New Testament outside the Gospels. These experiences have as their objects beings who are in heaven. In order to have these experiences, the seer must be caught up like the "man in Christ" who "was caught up to the third heaven" (II Cor. 12:2) and the author of Revelation who "in the Spirit on the Lord's day" beheld the furniture and personae in heaven (Rev. 1:10 ff.), or he must look into heaven like Stephen, who at the moment of his death saw "the heavens opened, and the Son of Man standing at the right hand of God" (Acts 7:56). This experience of occupants of heaven is the appropriate context for a correct understanding of the phenomenon of resurrection appearances in I Cor., ch. 15. The Jesus they saw was most probably in heaven and they saw him as a heavenly being. Still these heavenly circumstances did not obscure his identity as the Jesus from Nazareth whose career ended in crucifixion.

The second thing that tends to encumber our understanding of these primitive resurrection appearances is the difficulty moderns have with conceiving that such visionary experiences could have any more reality than a dream. We must recognize that this is our problem and that it was not a problem for the New Testament church at the time of Jesus' resurrection. Because an experience belonged to the category of visions of heavenly beings, it did not make that experience or the heavenly beings in it any less real to inhabitants of the Greco-Roman world. The words for "see" and "was seen" or "appeared" were not distinguishable from each other on the scale of objective reality. The beings in the heavenly visions were as real to first-century authors and readers of the New Testament as anyone they met in "common" life. The question was not whether such things could be, but only whether the witness was telling the truth.[10] Once belief in a future heavenly world was established, heavenly appearances followed naturally.

The first-generation New Testament church was content,

then, to base its faith on the appearances of a risen Jesus to Peter, the Twelve, and the others whom Paul added to the earliest tradition. These others were more than five hundred brethren, James, all the apostles, and Paul himself (I Cor. 15:6-8). It is difficult to specify the chronology of these official appearances except to say that Peter was the first witness and Paul the last. The confession gives no clear identification of the "five hundred brethren" or of "the apostles." Nor can we tell, except in the case of Paul, when or where the appearances took place. There is not enough evidence to equate the appearance to the five hundred with the experience of Pentecost recorded in Acts. All that is clear in this regard is that Paul expected his readers to know whom he meant. So it is reasonable to suppose that these appearances were familiar to the church, and that Paul's list was accepted as the complete official witness to Jesus' resurrection.

Though obviously known and accepted as complete, it is another question whether the early church found this witness entirely satisfying. One allusion to the list of appearances exposes the first anxiety we find connected with early belief in Jesus' resurrection. Paul felt compelled to observe about the more than five hundred brethren that most of them were still alive though some had died (I Cor. 15:6). This is a telltale indication that the church was already becoming anxious over the disappearance of the official witnesses to the ground of its faith. The church was beginning to wonder where it would stand when all the witnesses died. The matter was not yet serious enough for direct consideration. Presumably the return of Christ would remedy this situation before it overtook the church. But we know the Parousia did not provide the remedy. Looking back, we can recognize in this slight fissure the surface manifestation of a deep fault that will eventually so disturb the ground of resurrection faith that it will force the church to seek more solid footing.

However, all problems were not that far away. In the course of following Paul's attempt to solve the difficulty that the Corinthian church was having with the resurrection, we shall find confirmation of our preliminary understanding of the nature of the resurrection appearance as a heavenly phenomenon.

The Corinthians' difficulty was complex. Paul's side of the conversation assumed a curious combination of denials and admissions on the side of the Corinthian church. They believed that Jesus was raised from the dead—"so we preach and so you believed" (I Cor., 15:11)—but some said there was no *general* resurrection from the dead (v. 12b). At the same time they believed that there was some kind of life after death because they practiced substitute baptism on behalf of deceased members of the community (v. 29). Schmithals makes the most helpful suggestion for a coherent pattern of conviction that combines these three apparently mutually exclusive beliefs.[11] The Corinthian opponents were Gnostics or Proto-gnostics who believed in the resurrection of Jesus as the redeemer, but who anticipated for themselves a spiritual, disembodied afterlife on the basis of a regenerating union with the (mythically?) dying and rising Savior. In typical Gnostic fashion, they deplored fleshly, bodily existence and hoped to escape from it in the next life. They had heard Paul speak disparagingly of flesh and assumed their view of bodily existence was the same as Paul's view. "I tell you this, brethren: flesh and blood cannot inherit the kingdom of God." (V. 50.) But Paul disappointed them by teaching a general bodily resurrection that seemed to perpetuate the very fleshly existence they hoped by redemption finally to escape. In the mind of the Corinthians, bodily existence and fleshly existence were bound together.

Paul hoped to convince them of the plausibility of his own view by separating bodily existence and fleshly existence, and by maintaining that Christ's resurrection was not just a pattern for redemption but also a pattern for the future bodily afterlife of believers. He argued for this latter point in I Cor. 15:12–28. In Paul's mind, the general future resurrection and the resurrection of Jesus were so intimately bound together that to deny the general resurrection was to deny both the resurrection of

Jesus and any hope of future life.[12] Any other form of afterlife than a resurrection one was unthinkable to Paul, the ex-Pharisee. To believe in life after death was to believe in a resurrected life and a resurrected life was based on the bodily resurrection of Jesus.

In I Cor. 15:20 ff. Paul advanced his argument in a positive way. Christ's resurrection and the resurrection of believers were as related as the "first fruits" are to a full crop (vs. 23 ff.). The produce is all of one kind, and the firstfruits tell what the kind is.

In I Cor. 15:35 ff. Paul argued for the separation of the idea of bodily resurrection existence from fleshly existence. Using analogies, he pointed out that God provided two different kinds of bodies for each plant, the seed and the flower. So also in man there are two bodies, the seed body of earthly life and the flower body in resurrection.

I Corinthians 15:42–49 describe the two kinds of bodies. It is here that we find the most precise description in the New Testament of the resurrection mode of existence and, by implication, of the content of resurrection appearances. We must keep in mind that Paul's whole discussion was based upon the original official appearances of the resurrected Christ.

Paul compared the preresurrection body with the resurrection body by means of four pairs of opposing terms. The first term in each pair described the preresurrection body, the second term applied to the resurrection body. The pairs were: perishable/imperishable; dishonor/glory; weakness/power; physical/spiritual. Paul summed up the argument in I Cor. 15:44b: "If there is a physical body, there is also a spiritual body."

Paul's commentary confirms what we deduced from the resurrection confession itself. According to the pairs of descriptive terms, the resurrected Jesus was from heaven not from earth (I Cor. 15:48–49).

In the light of the Corinthians' difficulty understanding Paul, one final evaluation of the earliest church's view of Jesus' resurrection prepares us to move to the Gospels. Among people who were not protected by a Jewish heritage, the resurrection of Jesus confirmed the dualistic pessimism prevelant in Hellenistic culture. It must have seemed to the Corinthians that the message of the church was encouraging them in their opposition to life in the flesh. How could it be sinful to indulge bodily appetites when the body was not really important, having been declared obsolete by the resurrection of the Spirit? It is easy to see how any faith based on resurrection would confirm such antihistorical leanings. And by the same token, if the early church hoped to check the drift away from history that was natural to all its Hellenistic converts, it would need a more historical object of faith than the risen spiritual Lord of the earliest resurrection confession.

Mark

When we turn from the confession in I Cor., ch. 15, to Mark, we suddenly vault over thirty years or more of the first crucial years of the church. In Roman history it is the jump from Caligula to Vespasian. The change we observe in the form of resurrection witness is almost as striking as the difference between the characters of the two emperors—the one megalomaniac, the other restrained. We have dated Mark sometime shortly after A.D. 70. This results from the appropriate procedure that dates all apocalyptic literature by the last historical event discernible in its lists of predictions for the future. In Mark this event was the destruction of Jerusalem in the war with Rome in A.D. 70. Referring to the buildings of Jerusalem, Mark had Jesus say, "There will not be left here one stone upon another, that will not be thrown down."

The abrupt change in the nature of the material when we compare the earliest resurrection confession and the appearance stories of the first three Gospels can hardly be exaggerated.

There are two stages in the resurrection witness material: a suprahistorical stage and a historical one. In the letters, the risen Jesus appeared as a suprahistorical figure and the resurrection witnesses recorded a suprahistorical experience. The witness himself provided whatever history there is in the revelatory vision. In the historical stage, the risen Jesus shared at least some conditions of historical existence with the witnesses.

The suprahistorical stage is the earlier. As we have noted, most of the material in this period was confessional; e.g., Rom. 1:3–4; I Peter 3:18; I Tim. 3:16. Each of these confessions had "flesh" before resurrection and "spirit" afterward, so that any witness to Jesus as the resurrected one would need to be according to the Spirit; that is to say, it would need to be a suprahistorical perception.

On the other hand, Mark, Matthew, and Luke all begin with a historical incident—the empty tomb. When the resurrected one does appear we are suddenly confronted with a flesh and blood Jesus who even in his resurrected state belonged to the realm of material history. The empty tomb seems to be clearly intended as evidence of a resurrected Jesus that could stand the tests of historical criteria because in his resurrection he took his earthly body with him.

This is certainly an accurate estimate of the function of the empty tomb story in Matthew and Luke. I think, however, we must be more cautious when we deal with Mark. I shall attempt to show first that the empty tomb was not a piece of tradition that reflected pre-Marcan views but was rather Mark's own creation. Secondly, I shall attempt to show that it was not primarily a resurrection story that prepared the way for appearances of the risen Lord in a physical body. Instead I wish to contend that it was a translation story in resurrection guise. Readers tend to miss Mark's original point only because he was more subtle than we suppose and because it is difficult to refrain from supplying Mark with appearances from Matthew and Luke.

Martin Dibelius was typical of exegetes who judge that the story of the empty tomb rests upon tradition.[13] This was apparent in his classifying it as legend—"religious narrative of a saintly man in whose words and fate interest is taken." This takes into account certain suprahistorical embellishments but does not adequately challenge the historical core of the story. Moreover, Dibelius made the empty tomb story part of the larger passion-story cultus-legend which obviously reflects events that really took place. This has the effect of allowing the passion narrative to lend the empty tomb story an aura of historicity.

Dibelius advanced three arguments to show that the pericope of the empty tomb had a life of its own before its use by Mark. First, he said, "The fact that the women are mentioned at the beginning, superfluously after 15:47, seems to prove that it was originally independent of its connection in Mark."[14] Secondly, the command in ch. 16:7, "But go, tell his disciples and Peter that he is going before you into Galilee; there you will see him, as he told you," does not belong to the old legend, for here the Evangelist appeared to have joined the legend of the grave with the traditions already at hand in the church. Thirdly, the concluding words, "They [the women] said nothing to any one, for they were afraid," meant that the narrative of the empty tomb was still unknown in wide areas. Dibelius concluded that Mark did not create the story of the empty grave.

Taken one at a time and in reverse order, these arguments seem to me to indicate creation by Mark rather than his use of tradition.

The final statement that the women did not tell anyone suggests that Mark was apologizing for a story no one knew until he created it and published it to the church. The command to tell the disciples and Peter in Mark 16:7 shows that he was aware of the tradition of I Cor. 15:3–5 and that he ought to make Peter the first witness to Jesus' resurrection. To justify putting the women ahead of Peter, he then disregarded the command to the women to report their experience to the disciples. The common tradition could have had no way of knowing that the women witnessed the resurrection before Peter because "they said nothing to any one."

There is no way to judge from a formal analysis whether the command to tell Peter and the disciples to go to Galilee to see Jesus was an addition or an integral part of a traditional pericope. We shall defer judgment until other considerations lead more definitely to a conclusion. The story would make sense without the command, but then it would not fulfill the prediction of Mark 14:28, "But after I am raised up, I will go before you to Galilee."

To turn to Dibelius' second argument, the list of three women at the beginning of the story is redundant since they are already named in Mark 15:40 and v. 47. The repetition is not redundant. The point is that Mark named them three times in order for them to function as witnesses in a special way. In v. 40 they were looking on at the crucifixion. In v. 47 two of the three witnessed the burial. When they were named the third time, they witnessed the empty tomb. What was Mark doing? He placed the women at each of the decisive points of the traditional confession—crucified, buried, raised—to qualify them as witnesses comparable to Peter and the disciples in the usual tradition. According to Mark, the disciples disqualified themselves by fleeing (ch. 14:50) or denying him (vs. 66 ff.).[15]

Dibelius overlooked one other figure in the pericope Mark mentioned before. I am indebted to my colleague, Professor Waetjen, for this point. The young man inside the tomb who informed the women is the same young man who flees naked in Mark 14:51–52. Like the women he also functions as a witness to tie together the arrest and the empty tomb.

What we have observed so far from the evidence of editorial activity is not invalidated by the Greek of the last phrase, "for they were afraid." In Greek the order of words is the reverse of the English translation leaving the conjunction "for" as the final word of the story. Examples from classical authors, church fathers, and the papyri all point to the possibility of this word order.[16]

Lightfoot noted that it was customary for Mark to climax an incident with the impression it makes upon the observer. The empty tomb and the young man's announcement left the women in an appropriate state of awe at a divine revelation.[17]

A reinterpretation of the supposed evidence for tradition behind the story of the empty tomb has led us to the possibility at least that this was Mark's creation. Once we are open for that possibility, we can move on to ask why Mark might have composed it. As we seek to answer this question, Mark's unique posture toward the resurrection of Jesus begins to unfold and becomes a key to the theology of his Gospel.

Why did Mark compose the story of the empty tomb? It was not because his conception of resurrection bodies demanded this kind of evidence. Mark already explained his view of the ground of resurrection and of the nature of resurrection bodies in the controversy (Mark 12:18 ff. with Sadducees over the hypothetical case of the woman who survived seven husbands posed the problem of whose wife she would be in the resurrection. Jesus answered, "They neither marry nor are given in marriage, but are like angels in heaven." This shows that Mark did not have a materialistic view of the resurrection body which would require the use of the corpse from the tomb.

In the same pericope, Mark grounds belief in resurrection not on Jesus' resurrection but on scriptures and the power of God who is the God not of the dead but of the living. This controversy, not the empty tomb, was Mark's equivalent of I Cor., ch. 15. We must seek another content for the empty tomb than the doctrine of resurrection. What might it be?

Bickerman came closest to the truth in his article "Das leere Grab."[18] He classified the story as an *Entrückung*, or removal story, rather than a resurrection. His article provided ample instances in Hellenistic culture when a hero has been declared a hero by evidence of an empty grave. Rohde made it unavoidably plain that Hellenistic culture reserved a special fate for those considered more than mortal. "A grave is always necessary to fix the Hero at a definite place, or, at least, an 'empty tomb,' which sometimes had to do duty for a grave."[19]

The story of the boxer Kleomedes of Astypalaia is a pertinent illustration.[20] He killed his opponent in the 71st Olympic festival (486 B.C.) and, furious at being disqualified, returned home where in a fit of pique he collapsed the roof of a school upon the boys within. Seeking sanctuary in a temple of Athena, he hid in a chest. His pursuers broke open the chest and found it empty. An oracle explained that Kleomedes had become a hero. This carrying away of the hero fits Plato's theory that the peculiar property of divinity was to live forever in the indivisible unity of body and soul.[21]

Hellenistic stories like the one about Kleomedes probably explain one motive Mark had in composing the empty tomb story. Greco-Roman readers of Mark, for whose sake Mark has the centurion make the confession, Son of God (Mark 15:39), would have their expectations satisfied. A Son of God would be expected to be carried away at his burial as was claimed for some emperors.[22] Hellenistic removal stories also throw light on the command at the empty tomb to go see Jesus in Galilee. The spirits of heroes "were confined within the boundaries of their native country, the neighborhood of their graves or the site of their cult.[23] The angel at the tomb made a point of relating Jesus to Galilee by calling him Jesus of Nazareth. From a Hellenistic point of view, Jesus should return to his native territory upon "removal."

Mark may have composed the empty tomb story in part to satisfy Greco-Roman expectations aroused by his Son of God Christology. I doubt, however, that this was his main purpose. His main purpose, in my opinion, relates to his other more dominant Christological theme, the Son of Man.

Mark expected the coming of the Son of Man before the end of his generation (Mark 9:1). The juxtaposition of the coming of the Son of Man in ch. 8:38 with the coming of the Kingdom in ch. 9:1 was Mark's way of showing that they would occur together. And the coming of the Kingdom is the principal context for the whole of Mark which was why Mark opened Jesus' ministry with a summary to the effect that the Kingdom is at hand (ch. 1:15). There is more here than an attempt to report Jesus to us. In the opening summary of the ministry the nearness of the Kingdom was made equivalent to "believe in the gospel."

The nearness of the Kingdom was a possibly obsolete element in Jesus' preaching that Mark reaffirms in his reader's day. This would match the most probable historical setting of Mark. We have already noted that Mark wrote after the destruction of Jerusalem: "There will not be left one stone upon another, that will not be thrown down" (Mark 13:2). We know from the antiapocalyptic emphasis among Jews at Jamnia that the destruction of Jerusalem greatly excited apocalyptic expectation. If God had allowed the destruction of his Temple, it would have been a sign that his final intervention was near. Christians, who perhaps had begun to make some adjustments to a delay of the Parousia, would then recover their original intense expectation. Since Mark shared in this expectation and indeed encouraged it, we may reasonably expect that he wrote because he had some special light to throw on it. This special conviction about the immediate coming of the Kingdom and the Son of Man prompted the composition of the first Gospel and dictated its structure.

We are on the right track to this special conviction if we follow Bickerman's lead but place it in the setting of Mark's theology instead of some general framework of Hellenistic culture. The empty tomb story was most probably a translation story. In fact it may be most accurate to call it an antiresurrection story. Assuming that Mark ends at ch. 16:8, the most obvious thing about the empty tomb story compared to resurrection tradition is that it avoided the resurrected Jesus. It is as though Mark felt that Jesus' appearances to the church distracted the church from something more important; i.e., the

Parousia. As we see in Paul, the presence of the risen Lord in some measure compensated for and made tolerable a delay in his return. Mark wished to eliminate that substitute for the Parousia.

Mark gave believers little encouragement for spiritual experiences of any kind. In place of the presence of the risen Jesus, Mark simply and strikingly affirmed his absence.

What did translation mean positively in Mark's thought? The transfiguration story suggests the answer (Mark 9:2-8). On a high mountain Moses and Elijah "appeared" to Jesus, Peter, James, and John. Mark's word for "appeared" is the same one used in I Cor., ch. 15, and it is used the same way to describe a vision of heavenly beings. Since the conversation between Jesus and Moses and Elijah was not reported, we are left to deduce the meaning of this group. The one thing Elijah and Moses had in common with Jesus was that they too were translated. Though the Biblical account had Moses die, this does not prevent legend honoring him with translation and no grave. Deuteronomy had already set the stage. "So Moses . . . died there in the land of Moab . . . ; but no man knows the place of his burial to this day." (Deut. 34:5-6.) Josephus' account was typical of the way the mystery of burial developed into a translation.

> And while he (Moses) bade farewell to Eleazar and Joshua and was yet communing with them, a cloud of a sudden descended upon him and he disappeared in a ravine. But he has written of himself in the sacred books that he died, for fear lest they should venture to say that by reason of his surpassing virtue he had gone back to the Deity.[24]

The translation of Elijah is familiar (II Kings 2:11-12). On the mountain, Mark offered both Moses and Elijah as models for understanding Jesus' career; however, he actually developed only one of these models—Elijah. Elijah provided the framework in which Mark asked his readers to understand Jesus.

Elijah had two earthly careers. His first career was as the Old

Testament prophet. His second career according to Mark was as John the Baptist. This is implied in Mark 9:13: "Elijah has come, and they did to him whatever they pleased." Mark described John's clothing to match Elijah's (ch. 1:6). John appeared by the Jordan because this was where Elijah disappeared. Elijah's second career as John was the sign that the eschatological time was at hand. Following the model of Elijah, Mark created a double career for the Son of Man. The first career was the ministry of Jesus—he forgave sin as the Son of Man (ch. 2:10), set aside the Sabbath as the Son of Man (v. 28), and died as Son of Man (ch. 9:12). The second career would be as the traditional Son of Man come in power and glory (chs. 9:1; 13:26; 14:62). The appropriate transition between careers must be a translation. This is what Mark made out of the resurrection tradition (chs. 9:9, 31; 10:33). Even the three days between crucifixion and the futile search for Jesus by the women now took on new meaning. Not satisfied that Elilah was gone, men from his school of prophets prevailed upon his successor Elisha to let them search for him. "They sent therefore fifty men; and for three days they sought him but did not find him." (II Kings 2:17.)

If this is a correct analysis, Mark's special contribution to the eschatological crisis after A.D. 70 was his conviction that the resurrected Messiah should be replaced by a translated and returning Son of Man who would have an earthly career analogous to his first career as Jesus of Nazareth, only this time with the power and glory of the Kingdom of God. In contrast to the movement of the interest of the church toward heaven, Mark wished to refocus attention to earth.

Herod's fear that Jesus was John returned after his death showed that reappearance was a comfortable idea for Mark's cultural milieu (Mark 6:6). Alexander the Great and Nero were both expected to enjoy second careers.[25]

Mark's interest in working out eschatology on earth was so strong that he even had a theory about the geography of fulfillment.[26] This is the meaning of Mark 16:7, "But go tell his disciples and Peter that he is going before you to Galilee; there you will see him, as he told you." These directions were intended for Mark's readers, not the women or the disciples who never got this message. In keeping with the setting of Mark this word was for the church that had fled Jerusalem after the year 70 and was wondering whether or not to return. In the story of the empty tomb Mark was saying, "Do not return to Jerusalem, but go to Galilee where the Son of Man will soon begin his second career."

How did Mark arrive at Galilee as the place? Probably he interpreted the destruction of Jerusalem as a providential sign that God had abandoned the traditional site of the eschatological drama. Instead of Judaism and its homeland, Judea, God chose the land of the Son of Man as the focus of the end. What location was especially appropriate to him? Jesus was from Nazareth in Galilee. The new holy place must be Galilee. Mark followed this same kind of geographical consideration in the beginning of his Gospel.[27] John appears at the Jordan because Elijah was translated near the Jordan. The geography of the first career dictated the location of the second.

If we have understood Mark correctly, it is a serious misunderstanding of Matthew and Luke to suppose they moved in the same direction as Mark. Matthew and Luke used Mark's story of the empty tomb as though he offered it as the ground for belief in the resurrected Jesus. Following this false lead, they wrote Gospels that took the historicity of Jesus and injected it into his resurrection in order to give resurrection enough rigidity to support the faith of the church. By contrast, Mark wished to reinterpret the traditional resurrection. Rather than present it as quasi-history, he saw it as a transition from the real history of Jesus' first career to an equally historical second career. And Mark's conviction about this second career compelled him to create a fitting first career.

Our investigation of Mark's supposed resurrection story has led us to confirm the interpretation of Lohmeyer, Lightfoot, and others—Mark intended to end his Gospel with ch. 16:8.

and that the Gospel finally points to the return of the Son of Man and not to resurrection appearances. Mark was a more subtle, creative theologian than has yet been realized. He was so subtle that his imitation of certain traditional elements of early church resurrection conviction mislead us into supposing he represented no departure from earliest tradition. He took the traditional word for "he was raised" (I Cor. 15:4) and used it not as an equivalent of the precise word for "resurrection" (v. 12) but, following another connotation, used it for the "raising up" or "lifting up" of translation. Each time Jesus predicted his "resurrection" from Mark's point of view, he was actually predicting his translation.

Our primary interest is not, however, the subtlety of Mark or even the structure of his theology. We finally want to know which early church attitude toward Jesus' resurrection Mark represented. The first significance of Mark is that he represented a general recovery of confidence in the initial posture of the primitive church. The earliest church believed in the immediate return of Christ or at least within the lifetime of the first generation of Christians. By A.D. 70 that first generation had practically disappeared. Its passing worried the Thessalonian Christians. Paul betrayed his consciousness of time running out with his notice that some of the more than five hundred resurrection witnesses had died. By the year 70, James, Peter, Paul, and presumably most of the original church leaders had died. The realization of a delay of the return of Christ must have been pressing itself upon this rising second-generation church. Mark temporarily saved that church from facing up to the crisis. The destruction of Jerusalem was distracting enough to permit a persuasive case to be made by Mark.

By meeting the crisis at the delay of the Parousia, we may reasonably suppose he had also fended off an accompanying crisis in resurrection belief. Now that all the original, official witnesses to Jesus' resurrection have died, how will the rising church ground its inherited resurrection conviction? This particular frustration from lack of firsthand visual contact with the risen Lord would soon be repaired by his full manifestation upon earth as Son of Man. Because the church could be sure of meeting its risen Lord soon, it could bear the anxiety of not seeing him now.

But the ground for reassurance that Jesus would return had shifted. As we have noted, the return of Jesus was originally grounded in the resurrection visions that identified the risen Jesus as the Son of Man. When that was not a privilege open to the church, Mark showed that the church preferred something historically more secure than the tradition of the heavenly visions. It is at this point that the ministry of Jesus first took on decisive importance to the church. What used to be proved by heavenly visions of a spiritual Lord must now be shown to have firmer undergirding in the ministry of Jesus. Mark substituted the appearances of the ministry for the appearances of the resurrection.

But in order to use Jesus for this new purpose, his earthly career must be given definite content. It must now, for the first time, become a "life" with enough thematic direction to point the way to a parousia and to make it believable in spite of disappointing delay. The genius of Mark is that he molded such a life. It is a monument to the credibility of his work that Matthew and Luke were compelled to take his mold into account. And although we must be careful not to claim too much for Mark (someone may have pioneered the molding of a "life" of Jesus that Mark used). Mark was the one that survived as the model.

His empty tomb story is the surest proof we have that Mark did his work in an atmosphere of uncertainty about the resurrection of Jesus. He arranged a witness to the resurrection of Jesus without finding it necessary to exhibit the risen one. Comparison with the earliest resurrection witness that depended upon appearance highlights how great a reversal this was.

This, of course, does not mean that resurrection conviction played little or no part in Mark's creation of the career of Jesus, the coming Son of Man. Without the experience of the appearances to the church, Mark would never have been able to identify Jesus as the Son of Man. Mark was able to accept the fruit of his heritage as apart from ground that heritage brought with it.

This is of supreme significance to the evaluation of the roles which the Gospels assigned to Jesus. In Mark, and as we shall see in Matthew and Luke, the role assigned to Jesus did not arise out of his ministry. The role grew out of a prior convictional posture toward Jesus which each Gospel author received from a resurrection-centered church but which he had then to shape and ground according to the new situation in which he lived.

The pictures we have of Jesus' career are conditional and timely. They are products of a particular situation. As the situation changes, the picture of Jesus necessarily changes.

Matthew

With Matthew the situation changed. He was willing to return to the traditional center of the earliest church and make the resurrection of Jesus, and more especially *appearances* of the risen Lord, the ground of his solution to his situation. Like Mark's situation, it was new—new compared to the earliest church and new compared to Mark. The new situation forced a new form of resurrection conviction and with it a new form for the ministry of Jesus. The newness of Matthew shows best if we take the same route with him we have with Mark, that is, if we follow the development of the way resurrection appearances were treated.

With Matthew we meet resurrection appearances once again after Mark's studious avoidance of them. But Matthew also disturbed the traditional order of appearances in I Cor. 15:3–5. The first persons to see Jesus were the women coming from the empty tomb. "And behold, Jesus met them and said, 'Hail!' And they came up and took hold of his feet and worshiped him." (Matt. 28:9.) There is no individual appearance to Peter at all. Equally interesting is that Peter is even eliminated from the angel's charge to the women. Where Mark reads, "Go, tell his disciples and Peter," Matthew has the angel say, "Go quickly and tell his disciples" (Mark 16:7; Matt. 28:7). This does not mean that Matthew intended to detract from Peter's traditional primacy within the resurrection appearances. Actually he wished to establish Peter's primacy. But in Matthew's opinion there was a more important ground for Peter's primacy than could be trusted to appearances of the resurrected Jesus. Instead, the earthly Jesus guaranteed Peter's primacy by appointing him the rock and final arbiter in matters of church discipline (Matt. 16:18–20).

We see here the same movement away from resurrection to Jesus that we noticed in Mark. This movement is especially obvious in Matthew because it concerns a subject of special interest to Matthew—church order—and also because it is probable that Matthew composed the section on Peter's primacy rather than using a resurrection tradition that was already at hand.[28] This shows how determined Matthew was to retain the resurrection tradition without being too exclusively at its mercy.

We can only guess why Mark found resurrection appearances troublesome and preferred to avoid them. In Matthew, it is clearer why conviction about Jesus' resurrection is problematic. A special attack had been mounted directly against the church's witness to the resurrection and Matthew was on the defensive. Far from being a simple statement of conviction, Matthew's resurrection story is largely an apology.

The antagonists in this matter were the chief priests and Pharisees who prevailed on Pilate to set a guard at the tomb lest the disciples steal Jesus' body and stage a fraudulent resurrection (Matt. 27:62–66). Then according to Matthew, the chief priests and elders bribed the soldiers who witnessed the resurrection to say the disciples stole the body, "and this story has been spread among the Jews to this day." The same leaders

of the Jews who were made responsible for the unjust crucifixion of Jesus were also made responsible for attacking the doctrine of Jesus' resurrection. Matthew held the leaders primarily
responsible, but the situation had deteriorated farther than
that. Not only had the leaders erred, but Matthew's church
was conscious of existing over against "the Jews." The separation between Judaism and Christianity had taken place. As we
shall describe in some detail in the next chapter, Judaism had
begun now to attack the distinctive doctrines of Christianity
including the resurrection of Jesus.

The guards were symptomatic of this new Jewish opposition
to Christianity. To combat the empty tomb, Judaism had
brought the guards as counterwitness. In some fashion they
were used to witness to the theft of Jesus' corpse. Perhaps Matthew reported the countertestimony accurately: "His disciples
came by night and stole him away while we were asleep." If
so, he found what he considered a telling flaw in the witness of
the soldiers; namely, they would not incriminate themselves by
an admission that they fell asleep on duty without being bribed.
And furthermore, soldiers would have been punished for such
an admission unless the Jews had intervened with the authorities. Matthew countered with the bribe by "the chief priests"
(Matt. 28:11–12) and the promise of intervention by them in
case word got to Pilate, "the governor" (ch. 27:2).

A second polemic note is the repetition of Mark's emphasis
on Galilee. Matthew had both the angel and the risen Jesus in-
struct the women to tell the disciples that the resurrection appearance would be in Galilee. This simple following of Mark's
geography did not match Mark's intention. Mark meant the return of the Son of Man. Matthew thought of traditional appearances. But Matthew no doubt had at least the negative purpose
in common with Mark, namely, to shift the scene of revelation
from Jerusalem. Jerusalem had forfeited any right to importance because it had always rejected the prophets and messengers whom God had sent to it (Matt. 23:37–39). Matthew
had Jesus predict specifically that Jerusalem might not be the

scene of the appearances. "For I tell you [Jerusalem], you will not see me again, until you say, 'Blessed is he who comes in the name of the Lord.'" (V. 39.) The saying parallels the saying of the risen Jesus to the women, "Tell my brethren to go to Galilee, and there they will see me." Matthew did not understand Mark's reason for directing attention to Galilee as the homeland of Jesus' first career which dictated the location of his second career as Son of Man. Accordingly, Matthew dropped "Nazareth" in the angel's word to the women at the tomb. Instead of, "You seek Jesus of Nazareth," Matthew had, "You seek Jesus."

The third evidence of a polemic purpose is Matthew's modification of the role of the women. Unless they saw the risen Jesus, they were no help against the countercharge that the disciples stole the body. Matthew granted them an appearance in spite of the fact that there it contradicted both the traditional primacy of Peter's and Matthew's rejection of Jerusalem as a site for "seeing" Jesus. From our observations so far, we can see that Matthew had asserted his editorial role as he felt necessary.

These polemic thrusts amount to mere embellishments compared with the new thrust which Matthew imparted to resurrection witness. We have seen that Mark did not intend to set the stage for a physical resurrection with the empty tomb, or even to use it to buttress the reliability of Jesus' resurrection. Now we are in a position to see that Matthew, contrary to Mark, intended to prove the resurrection of a material-bodily Jesus by the empty tomb. This necessity of a material resurrection was laid on Matthew for two reasons: Matthew's view of resurrection called for it and the situation within the church required it.

Matthew reproduced Mark's controversy over the woman who had seven husbands in succession. He agreed that "in the resurrection they neither marry nor are given in marriage, but are like angels in heaven. But since this contains no material special to Matthew, it gives us no clue to Matthew's particular view. For this we must turn to Matthew's stories of the resurrections of the saints at the time of the crucifixion and the saying about Jonah. In these we have an indication of the perspective with which Matthew approaches Jesus' resurrection.

In the story of the rising of the saints at the crucifixion, Matthew drew attention to the bodies of the saints so that a physical entity was almost required to carry out the action. The "saints" were not the subject of resurrection but, rather, their *bodies*—"many bodies of the saints . . . were raised" (Matt. 27:52). To accommodate these apparently physical bodies, the tombs "were opened" (v. 52) and they "went out" (v. 53) as any historical person might. They "appeared" to many in the city. Matthew used a different word for "appeared" than the tradition of the confession in I Cor., ch. 15. Perhaps Matthew chose his word to emphasize the historical character of the appearances in contrast to the traditional word with its vision associations. Matthew was setting the stage for a physical resurrection of Jesus.

Matthew's use of the Jonah story moved in the same direction. "For as Jonah was three days and three nights in the belly of the whale, so will the Son of man be three days and three nights in the heart of the earth." (Matt. 12:40.) The main point was to predict the three-day period between crucifixion and resurrection. But this comparison with Jonah clearly implied a body that was the same after resurrection as before, and that would not come from heaven but out of the earth where it was buried.

So when Matthew described Jesus' resurrection, he followed through with his conception. The angel pointed to the place in the tomb not where Jesus was placed but where he lay—where he resided until raised as Matt. 12:40 specified. The climax of his physical resurrection was in the appearance to the women: "And they came up and *took hold of his feet*" (italics added).

This text marks the watershed between the church's traditional witness to a resurrection of Jesus in a heavenly, spiritual body and its new attempt to historicize the resurrection with an earthly, material body.

Matthew's history-making shift in the form of resurrection witness was most likely not merely his preference for the physical over the spiritual. He was content enough to use Mark in comparing resurrected believers to angels in the story of the woman with seven husbands. His shift to a physical resurrection was in response to an inner-churchly situation of resurrection doubt. This was serious doubt—doubt in the face of the appearance of the risen Jesus; doubt among the eleven disciples. "And when they saw him they worshiped him; but some doubted." What is most remarkable, Matthew closed his Gospel with the doubt among the Eleven unresolved! What could Matthew be saying but that some people in the church found the resurrection of Jesus unconvincing or at least that it was no longer the ground of faith for some?[29]

This doubt motif was the symbol of the new situation in which Matthew composed his Gospel. It symbolized the need to seek a firmer ground for belief. Mark found this new ground in the nearness of the Parousia buttressed by a career of Jesus that called for a second career as the Son of Man. Matthew moved in a different direction. Mark's option was not really available to Matthew since Mark's prediction of the Parousia failed to come true.[30] Matthew showed his new ground for faith in the first resurrection incident he portrayed. That incident was the going forth of the saints from their tombs. The death of Jesus occasioned this event. It was also the occasion for the tearing of the Temple curtain that symbolized the end of the Temple. It was also the occasion of the earthquake as a sign of eschatological significance. The death of Jesus was the new saving event to which Matthew moved as a result of the doubt cast upon Jesus' resurrection outside the church and within.

Matthew was moving toward a history that would steady the church in its new existence independent of Judaism and allay its anxiety over the resurrection appearances. Matthew buttressed the empty tomb evidence as best he could by injecting as much material-bodily historicity into it as possible. But if this was not satisfying to everyone in the church, there was an alternative. The alternative was the death of Jesus.

This death called for a life in which death itself had particular redemptive significance. Consequently Matthew committed himself to constructing a "life" for Jesus. He had to show that Jesus' teaching and miracles established him as the righteous one who, in his final, God-ordained act of obedience, fulfilled the way to salvation.[31] In Matthew for the first time Jesus provided the context of individual and communal life which had to reckon on continuing in history. Mark revealed Jesus as the Son of Man with his prescriptions for repentance in preparation for the return. He did not address himself to the problems of an enduring church. But Matthew portrayed Jesus as teacher and rabbi who defined the will of God in terms of law with such authority that he became Lord to the believing disciple.[32] He was ministering to a community that was decisively Jewish and its need for a way of life could only be satisfied by some interpretation of law. But more than that, there were constrictions in this cultural model that had to be transcended. It is in this connection that Matthew put Jesus' resurrection to positive use.

The commission on the mountain in Galilee was Matthew's way of escaping the bonds of Jewish culture. If Jesus had been called "teacher" and "rabbi," the danger existed of classifying his teaching as just one more element in the accumulating body of rabbinic tradition. At most, such a special tradition might have gained the dignity of a school, like Hillel or Schammai, at least it might have been cited as the peculiar teaching of a splinter sect. But, as Matthew obviously intended in the Sermon on the Mount, Jesus' teaching was the definitive interpretation of God's law superseding all past and future interpretations. Unlike any rabbi, Jesus had the all-encompassing authority of the exalted Son of Man. "All authority in heaven and on earth has been given to me." (Matt. 28:18.)[33]

Furthermore, Jesus' teaching transcended all other interpretations of the will of God because Jesus was continually present in the obedient community through the teaching and observance of his commandments until the end of the age. This was Matthew's solution to the absence of Jesus. It served as a substitute for resurrection appearances.[34] Matthew was employing the traditional Jewish concept of the Shekinah of God present in the Torah, but now adapted it to Jesus and his teaching.[35]

Not only did the teaching of Jesus transcend the limits of the rabbinic traditions, according to Matthew it also transcended the Jewish community. The will of God in Jesus' teaching was designed for all mankind. Through baptism and obedience to Jesus' commandments, all men could now become members of God's people; that is, disciples.

Finally, the concluding appearance story in Matthew granted to Jesus, the exalted Son, a dignity peculiar to the church's understanding of him, "baptizing them in the name of the Father and of the Son and of the Holy Spirit." Placing Jesus between the Father and the Spirit and worshiping him ("and when they saw him they worshiped him") raised Jesus above any competitive figure in Jewish tradition.[36]

This scene of the appearance of the risen Jesus and the commission to the nations was the climax of Matthew's theological creation. Surely that is what it was—his creation.[37] Like Mark, Matthew accepted the tradition of the resurrection only to rework it in accordance with his community's needs and his own theological bent. Mark moved on to the Parousia. Matthew moved back to the crucifixion. But Matthew also moved into the future of the congregation. In the teaching and accepting of Jesus' commands as the finally authoritative will of God, the congregation experienced the continuing presence of Jesus. What form would this authoritative teaching have in the continuing life of the congregation? Matthew created a life of Jesus to provide the answer. Matthew was the first New Testament author to create a form of Christianity in which Jesus of Nazareth functions as the continuing norm for the life of a church that reckons on a continuing world. Considering that this form of Christianity has dominated the history of Christianity, Matthew deserves recognition as the church's most influential theologian.

Luke

The development of the earliest church finds its completion in Luke. He is the theologian in the early church who was able to place Jesus in the center of the church's understanding of God's saving authority and at the same time manage to arrange all other theological and historical considerations accordingly. But because this center of Luke's theology belonged to a classical past, the danger loomed of Jesus becoming remote. Luke's handling of the resurrection tradition shows how his theology developed.

After Mark and Matthew, the empty tomb had almost supplanted the earliest confessional witness to the resurrection appearances. The story had found a firm place in churchly tradition. In Mark the women told no one, in Matthew they told the disciples, in Luke they told not only the Eleven but all the rest. Luke dealt with the empty tomb as if the incident was embarrassing to him.

The record of the disciples' reaction to the women's report conveyed Luke's estimate of its worth: "These words seemed to them an idle tale, and they did not believe them" (Luke 24:11). Luke was saying that the empty tomb no longer carried enough weight to convince the church that Jesus was raised from the dead.

One element in the story conflicted with Luke's theological interest in preserving the continuity between Judaism and Christianity. In Mark and Matthew, the story diverted attention from Jerusalem by directing the disciples to go to Galilee for the appearances. This was a judgment against Jerusalem. In order to reinstate Jerusalem as the center of the Christian revelation, Luke kept the reference to Galilee, but changed its meaning. Instead of "He is going before you to Galilee," Luke put, "While he was still in Galilee" (Luke 24:6), and retained Jerusalem as the place of the resurrection appearances. This is important in Luke's scheme of holy geography which begins in Jerusalem and moves through Samaria to the end of the earth (Luke 24:47; Acts 1:8).

Another aspect of Luke's account of the empty tomb expressing a theme of his theology was the connection the story made with arrest, crucifixion, and resurrection. "Remember how he told you . . . that the Son of man must be delivered into the hands of sinful men, and be crucified, and on the third day rise." (Luke 24:6–7.) All these events were foreknown by the Son of Man so that they unfold as the fulfillment of his promise. This promise and fulfillment scheme was basic to Luke's theology, especially in connection with the promises of scripture. Here Jesus stood in place of scripture. Later we shall see that the disciples should have expected all this from reading scripture. It is also important to note that Luke tied the crucifixion and resurrection together. They were practically one event for Luke.

Luke made a modification to Mark and Matthew that showed he was shy of using the empty tomb as evidence for Jesus' resurrection. When Mark and Matthew have the messengers announce the resurrection of Jesus, they called attention to the place where his body had been placed, "See the place where they laid him" (Mark 16:6); "Come, see the place where he lay" (Matt. 28:6). Luke has the simple announcement that Jesus is alive coupled with a rebuke for looking for him at the tomb: "Why do you seek the living among the dead?" (Luke 24:5). Having exposed the limitations of the empty tomb as a ground for belief in the resurrection of Jesus, Luke hastened to present what he thought was the appropriate ground in the very next story.

The story of the two apostles on the road to Emmaus was an exposition of Luke's solution to his church's problem with resurrection. We can gather by implication what the problem was. His church, represented by Cleopas and his companion, could not find assurance of Jesus' resurrection either from the empty tomb or from the tradition of the appearance to Peter. They could not believe the women's witness to the empty tomb even when confirmed by the disciples because, as they explain, there was no appearance: "But him they did not see" (Luke 24:24). The traditional appearance to Peter had no more effect upon "the eleven . . . and those who were with them" than the confirmed report of the empty tomb. "And they rose that same hour and returned to Jerusalem; and they found the eleven gathered together and those who were with them, who said, 'The Lord has risen indeed, and has appeared to Simon!' " "The eleven" and their companions must represent the unconvinced church of Luke. It would be a complete contradiction of logic and the tradition we have reviewed to suppose that the confirmed empty tomb and Peter's testimony could have had no effect in the church. The more reasonable explanation is that they had no decisive effect in Luke's church. In Luke's opinion, some other kind of testimony must confirm tradition before the church could be secure in its inherited confession that Jesus was raised.

The concluding verse of the section summarizes the decisive points of testimony for Luke. "Then they told what had happened on the road, and how he was known to them in the breaking of the bread." (Luke 24:35.) The first decisive point of testimony was the happening on the road. The climax of this legendary narrative was the rebuke given Cleopas and his friend. They were not rebuked for not believing the women from the empty tomb and the angel's message, nor for not believing the others who confirmed the women's report. They were rebuked for not believing the prophets. For the prophets, including Moses, according to Luke's theology, anticipated the death and resurrection of Jesus and, if they had believed the prophets, they would easily have believed the report of the traditional witnesses. "O foolish men, and slow of heart to believe all that the prophets have spoken! Was it not necessary that the Christ should suffer these things and enter into his glory?" (Luke 24:25–26.) Then followed Jesus' interpretation from "all the scriptures" of those necessary events.

Luke's point was obvious. At the time of his writing, the church had developed a detailed exposition of the Old Testament that found texts for each of the signal events in Jesus' career. The church had taken possession of the Old Testament. It argued that Judaism does not really understand it. This attitude was familiar in the church fathers, for instance, Justin Martyr with whom Luke shows special affinity.[38]

For an understanding of the relation between Jesus' resurrection and the composition of Luke, it is important to note who explained the Old Testament. It was Jesus, before he was recognized in his risen glory. The implication was obvious. Luke had written a life of Jesus for the express purpose of showing the connection between the scriptures and Jesus' life, and Jesus himself was the one throughout the Gospel who provided the Old Testament reference. The first incident in Luke's Gospel was a perfect illustration. Instead of beginning his ministry with the traditional message which Mark and Matthew attributed to him, Luke had Jesus, in his home synagogue, read a passage from Isaiah that amounted to a summary of Jesus' whole ministry. Hans Conzelmann and Paul Schubert both document this major motif in Luke's theology.[39]

The second decisive testimony that finally confirmed the traditional witness to Jesus' resurrection was symbolized by the meal experience of Cleopas and his companion. They received the revelation that this was Jesus alive after his death at a special moment. "When he was at table with them, he took the bread and blessed, and broke it, and gave it to them. And their eyes were opened and they recognized him." (Luke 24:30–31.) A comparison of this meal with Luke's account of the institution of the Lord's Supper in Luke, ch. 22, makes clear that Luke intended this meal to stand for the sacrament. In Luke only the bread had the sacramental word attached to it, which explains why the bread had the power to reveal Jesus apart from a cup.

Luke was offering his unbelieving church an experience of the presence of the risen Jesus in the celebration of the Lord's Supper, an experience that had the power to confirm the traditional reports of the empty tomb and of the appearances—at least of the appearance to Peter.

Now Luke was ready to repeat the traditional appearance to the disciples, but in the context of his own theological situation. Just as Matthew countered an attack upon the empty tomb, Luke met an objection to the content of the resurrection vision. When Jesus appeared he seemed to be a spirit and not fully real (Luke 24:37, 39). The troubled, questioning disciples must have represented Luke's community. He settled the question of the reality of the risen Jesus by presenting a physical body—the logical extension of Matthew's graspable Lord. An exhibition of flesh and bones and the eating of a piece of fish met all possible objections of a Docetic or Gnostic heresy (vs. 36–43).

Luke presented a complete reversal of the direction of the original resurrection witness recorded and explained by Paul. Paul's readers found a physical resurrection body unthinkable. By this time, Luke's community had found a spiritual body unreal.

Luke completed the physical appearance with three themes important to his theology. First he repeated the fulfillment-of-scripture theme enlarging the scriptural base to include not only the law of Moses and the prophets but also the psalms (Luke 24:44). Then he corrected the anti-Jerusalem element in Mark and Matthew by making Jerusalem the beginning point for the mission (v. 47), and by placing the disciples in the Temple (v. 53). The third theme was the anticipation of the "power from on high" which would equip the church for its mission once Jesus had ascended (v. 49).

Luke's handling of the resurrection was, of course, different from Mark's and Matthew's because it was continued in a second volume. The risen Jesus provided the transition from the Gospel to Acts. In Acts, the resurrection period was sharply terminated by an ascension. The meaning of the well-defined resurrection period was to qualify those who would be official apostles by virtue of belonging to the classic period that encompassed Jesus' preresurrection and postresurrection career on earth.[40] Those who were with Jesus until his death and whom he commissioned after the resurrection would provide the unrepeatable foundation period for the church that followed. The resurrection and ascension marked the climax of the central period in the scheme of redemptive history so carefully worked out by Luke.[41] The career of Jesus became the midpoint of redemptive history.

By the time we reach Luke, the career of Jesus that Luke's theology required was less directly related to Jesus' resurrection than was the case with Mark and Matthew. This is so because a life of Jesus had already been worked out and become the common possession of the church. Of course Luke made his own creative modification of it, but Jesus' career and ministry was part of Luke's heritage. So integral was the resurrection to the ministry that Jesus became an agent in his own resurrection—as he suffered so he rose (Luke 24:46).[42] But also, the ministry of Jesus had been so heavily employed by Mark and Matthew to buttress resurrection that Luke had to develop new ground to support both the redemptive claims for Jesus' ministry and the reliability of his resurrection. As we have seen, Luke found this final unassailable ground in part in the scriptures of the Old Testament. This was relatively unassailable ground because the church had so completely separated from Judaism that the only other community that understood the Old Testament and might object was effectively silenced by ostracism. As Luke, ch. 24, made clear, the Old Testament could only be understood from the churchly perspective of resurrection.[43]

Luke's other ground for resurrection conviction, the Lord's Supper, was also relatively safe. It was a self-authenticating experience that belonged to the church even more exclusively than the Old Testament. Luke found a way to ground the church's faith in Jesus as the resurrected one in ways that were external enough to the church to provide security and private enough to the church to be safe from outside attack.

But in the process something happened to both the resurrection and the ministry of Jesus. They were both relegated to the past. The resurrected, exalted Jesus was replaced in Luke's second volume by the activity of the Spirit.[44] The transfer is made when the exalted Lord pours out the gift of the Spirit in the church at Pentecost. In this way, Luke recognized the foundational importance of Jesus for the church and at the same time allowed the church to move beyond him.

Conclusion

We began with the question of the relation of the resurrection and the other world. It seemed that Christians were bound to the other world by the figure of a lord risen to that other world and fixed in it. Certainly this was the case in the earliest stage of resurrection witness. But Mark, Matthew, and Luke have shown that the risen Jesus could not remain fixed in the other world if the church was to continue to believe in the resurrection. It became necessary to create a Jesus with a historical career and to use the solidity of that history to give solidity to the resurrected Christ. In other words, to continue to believe in resurrection, the church moved its point of focus from the other world back into this world.

If we are to preserve resurrection faith in our time, we must follow the way pioneered by Mark, Matthew, and Luke. We must move in terms of the needs of the church in our culture, out of the other world back to this world. We must recover a historical Jesus.

Now we are clear that this is the path to follow. But before we begin to follow it, we must take fully into account the cultural factors that influenced the early church when it returned to the historical Jesus. Once we are aware of these cultural factors, we shall be able to escape captivity to them when we develop our own quest for a Jesus at home in this world.

NOTES

1. This assumes that the Gospels in the New Testament were composed during the period beginning with Mark after the destruction of the Temple and closing with Luke around 100. The evidence for the dating of each Gospel will appear as the setting of each Gospel unfolds. Much of the material that follows appeared in Neill Hamilton, "Resurrection Tradition and the Composition of Mark," *Journal of Biblical Literature*, Vol. 84, Part IV (1965), pp. 415 ff., and is used by permission of that journal.

2. A convenient summary of Paul's use of Jesus may be found in Rudolf Bultmann, "Die Bedeutung des geschichtlichen Jesus für die Theologie des Paulus," Glauben und Verstehen (Tübingen, 1954), Vol. I, pp. 188–213.

3. Helmut Köster, *Synoptische Überlieferung bei den apostolischen Vätern* (Berlin, 1957), pp. 266–267.

4. L. E. Wright, *Alterations of the Words of Jesus as Quoted in the Literature of the Second Century* (Harvard University Press, 1952).

5. Martin Kähler, *The So-called Historical Jesus and the Historic, Biblical Christ*, tr. and ed. by Carl E. Braaten (Fortress Press, 1964), p. 80, n. 11.

6. Paul Feine and Johannes Behm, *Einleitung in das neue Testament*, 12th ed., completely reworked by Werner G. Kümmel (Heidelberg, 1963), p. 206.

7. Joachim Jeremias, *The Eucharistic Words of Jesus*, tr. by Arnold Ehrhardt (The Macmillan Company, 1955), pp. 129–130.

8. Hans Grass, *Ostergeschehen und Osterberichte* (Göttingen, 1962), pp. 127 ff. Grass is the best and most recent treatment of the whole range of questions relating to resurrec-

tion witness in the New Testament. G. Koch, *Die Auferstehung Jesu Christi* (Tübingen, 1959), attempts to deal with the theological side of the question. Hans Conzelmann, "Auferstehung Christi in N.T.," *Die Religion in Geschichte und Gegenwart* (Tübingen, 1957), I, 698–700, is an excellent brief summary of the present situation in New Testament Studies. Maurice Goguel, *La foi à la résurrection de Jesus* (1933), often contains the best historicocritical judgments.

9. Cf. Grass, *op. cit.*, pp. 186–232, and W. Michaelis, "*óraō*," Gerhard Kittel, *Theologisches Wörterbuch zum Neuen Testament*, V, pp. 355 ff.

10. In the final chapter we shall attempt some evaluation of the witness to the resurrection appearances that will take into account the reservations many moderns have about heavenly visions. Suffice to observe now that the New Testament does not provide any direct help for problems its writers did not feel.

11. Walther Schmithals, *Die Gnosis in Korinth* (Göttingen, 1956), pp. 70 ff.

12. Paul may not have fully understood that for the Corinthians to deny the general resurrection was not to deny hope of life after death but to fend off the hated bodily existence in the flesh. Cf. Schmithals, *op. cit.*, p. 72.

13. Martin Dibelius, *From Tradition to Gospel*, tr. by B. L. Wolff (Charles Scribner's Sons, 1933), pp. 190 ff.

14. *Ibid.*, p. 190.

15. H. R. Lightfoot, *Locality and Doctrine* (New York, n.d.), pp. 26–27.

16. *Ibid.*, pp. 11–15.

17. *Ibid.*, p. 23, n. 1.

18. Elias Bickerman, "Das leere Grab," *Zeitschrift für die neutestamentliche Wissenschaft*, 23 (1924), pp. 281–291.

19. Erwin Rohde, *Psyche* (London: Routledge and Kegan Paul, 1925), p. 122.

20. *Ibid.*, p. 129.

21. *Ibid.*, p. 538.

22. *Ibid.*, p. 568, n. 107.

23. *Ibid.*, p. 134.

24. Josephus, *Antiquities* iv. 326; cf. iii, 97, and Philo, *Moses* II (291).

25. Rohde, *op. cit.*, p. 538.

26. Marxsen is prevented from detecting Mark's fundamental structure by beginning with opening incidents of the Gospel rather than the final and key story.

27. When in the discussion that follows, Matthew is spoken of as though he had been an individual, it may be more correct to think of him instead as a community expressing itself, more particularly perhaps a school, as has been suggested by a comparison of the way Matthew uses the Old Testament with the way the Qumran community used Habakkuk. Cf. Krister Stendahl, *The School of St. Matthew and Its Use of the Old Testament* (Uppsala, 1954), pp. 30–31.

28. George D. Kilpatrick, *The Origins of the Gospel According to Saint Matthew,* (Oxford University Press, 1946), p. 39, though he softens his judgment on p. 40. One might expect more decisiveness in the light of Kilpatrick's appreciation of the relation of Matthew to the break with Judaism (pp. 101 ff.). The appointment of Peter, like the tirade against the scribes and Pharisees in Matt., ch. 23, stems from this break. Cf Günther Bornkamm, in Günther Bornkamm, Gerhard Barth, and Heinz Joachim Held, *Tradition and Interpretation in Matthew* (The Westminster Press, 1963), pp. 45 ff.

29. Only Barth, *loc. cit.*, p. 132, and O. Michel, "Der Abschluss des Matthäusevangelium," *Evangelische Theologie*, 10 (1950/51), pp. 20 f., come close to granting enough weight to this doubt motif in Matthew. They both recognize it as Matthew's own creation. But Barth resolves the doubt too easily by suggesting that the Great Commission to the Gentiles is the way to overcome it. The doubt is not reported as overcome. Matthew accepted the doubt. This interpretation does not occur to commentators simply because it is unthinkable in a sacred book. For doubt's relation to faith and "little faith," cf. Held, *loc. cit.*, pp. 294–296.

30. Bornkamm, *loc. cit.*, p. 23 and p. 42, n. 3.

31. Cf. Barth, *loc. cit.*, pp. 143 ff.

32. Cf. Bornkamm, *loc. cit.*, pp. 41–42 where the relationships among "teacher," "rabbi," and "Lord" are explored.

33. Barth, *loc. cit.*, p. 133.

34. *Ibid.*, p. 135.

35. It would be clear from this alone that Matthew's community is willing to break with Judaism contra Bornkamm (*loc. cit.*, p. 39): "Matthew's Gospel confirms throughout that the congregation which he represented had not yet separated from Judaism."

36. Barth, *loc. cit.*, p. 131, n. 1; p. 133, n. 2.

37. We are at an advantage when dealing with Luke. Conzelmann has given such a penetrating analysis of the third Evangelist's thought that it has commanded a consensus among scholars. There is as yet no such generally accepted interpretation of Mark and Matthew. (Hans Conzelmann, *The Theology of St. Luke*, tr. by Geoffrey Buswell; Harper & Row, Publishers, Inc., 1961.)

38. J. C. O'Neill, *The Theology of Acts in Its Historical Setting* (London: S.P.C.K., 1961), pp. 10–15.

39. Paul Schubert, "The Structure and Significance of Luke 24," in *Neutestamentliche Studien für Rudolf Bultmann,* ed., Eltester (Berlin, 1957), pp. 178–185.

40. Conzelmann, *op. cit.*, p. 204.

41. *Ibid.*, pp. 175–176.

42. *Ibid.*, p. 162.

43. *Ibid.*, p. 176.

44. *Ibid.*, p. 190.

III

THE GREAT DIVORCE

We have seen the Jewish tradition taking shape in response to doubts about the adequacy of its own view of history. And we have seen Christian tradition taking shape in response to doubts about Jesus' resurrection. A resurrection faith that began with a minor role for the historical Jesus developed this history into a major basis for the thinking of the second-generation church.

While it was choosing the shape for Jesus' history, the church was also choosing its culture. There were two dominant cultures operative—Judaism and Hellenism. The early church at this point chose to reject its Jewish mother culture in favor of the culture of Rome. This choice of a new culture was a part of the development of Christianity into a religion distinct from Judaism. In the process, Judaism and Christianity became bitter enemies. This chapter will trace the separation of the two faiths and attempt to demonstrate how that separation became a decisive factor in shaping the church's view of Jesus' career.

However necessary this divorce may seem in retrospect, there is no way to soften the tragic consequences suffered by both communities. It is central to our whole investigation to note how that rift smothered one vigorous way of thinking about Jesus. And our purpose exactly is to revive that particular way.

The Crucifixion and the Political Situation of Judaism

Contrary to ancient assumptions within Christendom, the crucifixion of Jesus was not a hostile act of Judaism against Christianity. As we have observed in the preceding chapter, there was no distinctive Christian conviction prior to the resurrection witness. If some of our Gospel accounts seem at times to interpret the death of Jesus as a hostile act against Christianity, it is because these accounts were written *while* the divorce between the communities was taking place. It is important to clear away this obstacle to an understanding of the relation of Jesus' death to Judaism and then to take a good look at what really separated Judaism and Christianity.

The Romans executed Jesus as a political subversive. This is the point of the superscription they put upon his cross. If we can find some act of Jesus that could have been mistaken by Romans for political agitation, we can then lay the ghost of Jewish responsibility.

This act was the cleansing of the Temple. As I have argued elsewhere, the Temple contained the equivalent of a Jewish National Bank.[1] When Jesus upset the tables of the tellers of that bank, he seemed to be attacking the financial center of Roman Judea. Pilate could not ignore this threat to his position since he was especially responsible for the monies in his province. When Jesus superseded the economic function of the Temple, he must have appeared to the Romans to be taking upon himself the prerogatives of a new king of the Jews. Pilate could not ignore this seeming challenge.

Why did Jesus oppose this ancient and accepted economic function of the Temple? The answer follows from the main theme of his teaching—the nearness of the Kingdom. The approaching Kingdom suspended all competitive concern for the economic things of this world. But why bring this specifically to bear upon the Temple? Perhaps Jesus read Zech. 14:21: "And there shall no longer be a trader [Canaanite] in the house of the LORD of hosts on that day." In that case, this action could have been Jesus' way of preparing for or witnessing to the conditions of "that day" with respect to the Temple. He was acting in fulfillment of the obligation laid on him by Zechariah. And so it seems the death of Jesus of Nazareth had little to do with messianic claims or lack of messianic recognition. Rather, it was the pure tragedy of an eschatological prophet acting out his message and coming into collision with authorities who also had their obligations.[2]

This tragedy highlights the political situation of Judaism in Palestine. Due to the fact that Judaism belonged to two political communities—its own and Rome—it had constantly to protect itself from political disorder on two levels. At the time of the rise of the early church, the political situation within Judaism was in especially delicate balance. This balance was constantly threatened by a party within Judaism called the Zealots. They arose as a distinct group among the Pharisees about A.D. 6 or A.D. 7 when Quirinius, the legate of Syria, proceeded to take a census. Their basic conviction was exclusive allegiance to the dominion of God and rejection of all other political hegemony, especially that of Rome. Their program was revolution by force against Rome in order to usher in the end of history at which time God would then act on behalf of his people. The Zealot party stood for strict observance of the law and absolute separation from the whole Hellenistic, Gentile world. Its founder was Judas, the Galilean, and Galilee enjoyed the reputation of being the center of Zealot agitation.[3]

There is little doubt that Jesus and his Galilean followers were at least suspected of being Zealots. The Jewish accusation against Jesus amounted to identification as a Zealot in Roman eyes. Further, one of Jesus' followers, Simon, the Canaanite or Zealot, was or had been a Zealot. And it is probable that Judas was a Zealot (which would explain his disappointment with Jesus).[4] Jesus' concentration upon the imminent Kingdom of God coupled with the Galilean origin of his movement would lead many to associate it with insurrection, however mistaken this as a matter of fact was.

The whole period of the rise of the early church was set in this context of Zealot suspicion. Barabbas, for example, appears in the passion narrative as a rebel who was imprisoned in connection with an insurrection (Mark 15:7). Regardless of the historicity of Barabbas' role in the actual trial of Jesus, a Zealot connection for Barabbas fits the times for Mark's readers. In Luke, Jesus uses the suppression of what was probably a Zealot incident as an illustration in his teaching:[5] "There were some present at that very time who told him of the Galileans whose blood Pilate had mingled with their sacrifices" (Luke 13:1). Zealot activity was as distasteful to Pharisee, Sadducee, and Essene as it was to Rome, since all such strategy threatened to replace the privileges which Rome bestowed upon the Jews with punishment and vengeance. This fear was confirmed by the consequences of the Jewish rebellions in Palestine that occurred around A.D. 70 and A.D. 134.

Paul, the Jewish Theologian

If we hold the Zealot agitation in mind, it can explain the suspicion the early church aroused among some of their Jewish brethren. It does not mean that the early Christians were not Jews.

Paul is a case in point. Although his doctrine and the results of his mission eventually became the occasion for a Christian religion distinct from Judaism, his whole career unfolded inside Judaism and the background of his thinking was Jewish. Before Paul's conversion he was commissioned by Jewish authorities to apprehend Jews of Christian persuasion for discipline by the Jewish community. This showed that "Christians" were a party within Judaism subject to the police powers Jews had over other Jews by Roman permission (Gal. 1:13; Acts 8:3). Likewise, when Paul became a Christian Jew, he was subject to the discipline that Jewish laws specified for Jews. "Five times I have received at the hands of the Jews the forty lashes less one. . . . Once I was stoned." (II Cor. 11:24–25). In the same passage he insisted not only that he was a Jew but a Palestinian Jew (v. 22).[6] Paul's understanding of himself as a Christian "apostle" was probably a carry-over of the Jewish office of the same name. Men with this office held a commission to act for the high priest in the Diaspora.

It is true that Paul considered himself responsible to bring the gospel to the "uncircumcised" and "Gentiles" (Gal. 2:7-10). But the overwhelming evidence of the genuine letters of Paul shows that if Paul's converts were not circumcised Jews, they were Jews by persuasion who lived on the fringe of the Jewish community as "God-fearers" and had not yet taken the ritual steps necessary to become a convert, or who had entered the Jewish community of faith by baptism without circumcision.[7] Many of Paul's readers may have been so Hellenized and assimilated from a strict, conservative, Palestinian Pharisaic point of view—that is, from the point of view of the wing of the Pharisaic party to which Paul had belonged—that their orthodoxy was questionable. This did not, however, make them "Gentile" in the sense that their religious convictions were basically non-Jewish.

This argument must not be overdrawn. There was room in the Pauline church for converts who had little relation to Judaism and who began to share Jewish convictions for the first time through Paul's missionary activities. No doubt there were such in the Corinthian congregation.[8] The point is that Paul did not create a non-Jewish church. The "Christians" of Paul's time were a party within Judaism. In this Jewish party, which we call the early church, there were only Jews—some more Hellenized than others.[9] If this had not been the case, Paul would have been completely incomprehensible to his readers since the basis of each of his doctrines was a specifically Jewish conviction. This is perfectly obvious even in the case of the Pauline doctrine supposed to be most antithetical to Judaism—justification by faith.

As Paul developed the doctrine in his letter to the Romans, its whole context depended upon accepting the Jewish law as the definitive expression of the will of God. Without the law, sin would not be recognized as sin. And a consciousness of sin is the prerequisite of a longing for and understanding of redemption as Paul preached it. "If it had not been for the law, I should not have known sin. I should not have known what it is to covet if the law had not said, 'You shall not covet.' . . . Sin, finding opportunity in the commandment, deceived me and by it killed me. So the law is holy, and the commandment is holy and just and good." (Rom. 7:7–12.) Finally, to protect law from any derogation, he fixed upon sin as the cause of man's ethical failure, not law. Law was merely the occasion for exposing man's predicament before God. (Vs. 13–20.) Paul's doctrine of justification by faith cannot be relevant without a prior conviction about the sanctity of the law.

But the question immediately arises: Does not this doctrine of law destroy orthodox Judaism's respect for the saving role of law? The answer to this question is that there was no such thing as Orthodox Judaism with a saving role for law. Orthodox Judaism did not exist in Paul's day. That was established at Jamnia, as we shall see. To classify Paul's thought as non-Jewish according to this criterion is to judge a pre-Jamnian situation by post-Jamnian standards. This is historically unfair.

The necessity to substitute faith for law in Paul's doctrine of redemption is the same phenomenon we find in other admittedly Jewish literature such as IV Ezra. In this Jewish apocalpse, law was God's gift but condemned all mankind in a sinfulness law could not remedy. (IV Ezra 3:19 ff.; 9:31 ff.; 7:116–131.)[10] Just as Paul took his cue to man's predicament from apocalyptic thought, he worked out the solution to that predicament in the same context.

Paul's eschatology provides the key to his creativity and to the elements in his thought which eventually were declared non-Jewish. Paul believed in the doctrine of two ages. This present evil age would be ended by an act of God involving resurrection and judgment. This resurrection-judgment would usher in a new age and a new world. But as a result of the resurrection of Jesus, Paul was thrown into a situation not anticipated in any Jewish literature. The Messiah, or Son of Man, was raised separately from the general resurrection which traditionally was to begin the new age. The new age had already come in some sense, but the completion was still in the future. What was the believer's situation in this limbo between the times? It was here that Paul's Hellenistic background provided the elements of a solution not available in Jewish thought. He adopted the Hellenistic pattern of a dying and rising god to whom the devotee was bound in mystical union. This mystical union provided a spiritual power that enabled the believer to transcend the ethical limitations of ordinary worldly existence. The result was a Son of God Christology and a Spirit ethic that replaced law.

If Paul's doctrine of the Messiah and his ethics did not seem Jewish, it was not because he intended them to be otherwise. It was because the conviction that God had raised Jesus catapulted this Jew into a conceptual situation no Jew had imagined.[11] If, as a consequence, this Jew thought new thoughts with the aid of concepts from Hellenistic culture, they were still Jewish thoughts as far as Paul was concerned, for he continued to think of himself as a Jew.

What Paul did with Jesus is not completely without parallel in Jewish thought. Moses was elevated to comparable rank by other Jewish authors like Josephus and Philo, who were writing for Hellenistic audiences. We have already noted in Chapter II how the translation of Moses in Josephus implied superhuman status.[12] This is even more pronounced in Philo. He made Moses into a "divine man" and related mystical experience to ethical achievement so that in the mystical experience the law was necessarily fulfilled.[13] Paul's claims for the risen Jesus were no more extravagant than Philo's claims for Moses and the patriarchs. And Philo was certainly a Jew.

This, in my opinion, is adequate evidence that Paul's Christology stood well within the bounds of Hellenistic Judaism prior to Jamnia. And it is simply not accurate to say that Christian sources confirm the rejection of Paul's Christ soteriology by Hellenistic Jews.[14] All the Christian sources that record Jewish rejection of Paul's Christology are after Jamnia. Paul's correspondence shows that the trouble with fellow Jews came not from his doctrine of Christ but from his use of the law. We have already shown a Jewish parallel in IV Ezra of his attitude toward law. This means that only after Jamnia did Paul's way of thinking about Jesus become officially non-Jewish. This was, as we shall see, because "official" Judaism became anti-Hellenistic after Jamnia, just as "official" Christianity became anti-Jewish after Jamnia.

Certainly Paul considered himself Jewish and identified himself with the fate of his people, even to the extent of creating a special eschatological dispensation that would finally include all Israel in the mercy of God though they could not all respond to his message (Rom., chs. 9 to 11). And to the extent that he despaired of Israel, it was never directed against Israel as such but was a despair over a plight that the people of Israel shared with all mankind. Although his eschatology freed him from the law as a way of life, he still respected his Christian Jewish brethren who differed with him. He was willing to observe the law when he was with those whose consciences would be wounded by transgressing it. His position on law was not authoritarian but depended upon persuasion and consent (ch. 9:15). Paul went so far as to recognize that keeping all the provisions of the law was the way his more observant Christian Jewish brethren were expressing their faith in Jesus as Lord "He who observes the day, observes it in honor of the Lord. . . . He who abstains, abstains in honor of the Lord and gives thanks to God" (ch. 14:6). It is this more observant wing of Christian Judaism that is of special concern for our investigation because in it the Jewish appreciation of Jesus is best preserved.

But, before we turn to the less Hellenized Jewish wing of the earliest church, the points established so far need to be restated. Jesus was not put to death as a Jewish act directed against Christian convictions. His death was the death of a prophet caught in the political instability of Roman Judea. Jesus was a Jew at home with Jews.

The second point is that Paul was not a Christian instead of a Jew. He was a Jewish theologian exploring new ways of thinking about the Messiah.

The conclusion to be drawn from both these points is that we must cease to think of Jesus and Paul as exponents of anything but a Jewish way of believing and acting. Christianity ceased being Jewish only after Jesus and Paul.

These contentions are confirmed by the existence of an obviously proto-orthodox wing of the early church under the leadership of James.

James, the brother of Jesus, was the leader of observant Christian Judaism. He has his fixed place in the early resurrection tradition as the only one besides Peter to whom the risen Jesus appeared personally (I Cor. 15:7). Paul called him one of the "pillars" of the early church along with Peter and John; that is to say, first among the influential and recognized leaders (Gal. 2:9). This was his status seventeen years after Paul's conversion or about A.D. 50–52. Three years after Paul's conversion, James and Peter were the two apostles whom Paul met during his first visit to Jerusalem (ch. 1:18–19). James had, therefore, an initial and continuing role as leader in the early church. At each notice of him he is located in Jerusalem. Since Paul had to go to Jerusalem to authenticate his gospel with leaders there, this meant James was leader of Christian Judaism at its headquarters. The church was most at home among Jerusalem Jews and not in the Diaspora where Paul spent most of his time. All this supports the view that early Christian Judaism was predominantly observant or proto-orthodox.

Another notice of James shows how he exercised his leadership and to what ends: "Before certain men came from James, he [Peter] ate with the Gentiles; but when they came he drew back and separated himself, fearing the circumcision party"

(Gal. 2:12). In the undoubtedly pre-Jamnian literature of the New Testament this is the final notice we have of James, but it is especially rich with information.

The place of this encounter was Antioch—probably the nearest to Jerusalem of the large centers of Diaspora Judaism. The men who caused the stir between Peter and Paul "came from James." Jerusalem obviously had the same controlling authority for Christian Jews in the Diaspora as it had for all Diaspora Jews. But instead of the high priest exercising control, James was the comparable official for the church. He exercised his control, like the high priest, by sending his own "apostles" into the Diaspora to enforce the rulings of Jerusalem.[15] Paul had been exercising such an office for the Pharisaic wing of Judaism in pursuit of Christians on his way to Damascus (Acts 9:1 ff.).

Apparently word had come to Jerusalem that observant Christian Jews were giving up dietary provisions of the law to please Gentile converts. This had not been allowed by the Jerusalem meeting between James, Peter, and John on the one hand and Paul, Barnabas, and Titus on the other. The only concession the observant church had made was with regard to circumcision. Presumably the Gentile converts would become observant Jews in other respects. James sent his men probably to enforce this observance in accordance with the agreement. This matches Paul's interpretation of their action, for the charge he made against Peter was that, by compelling the return of the observance of dietary laws, he was compelling Gentiles to live like Jews (Gal. 2:14). And we must assume that because this was the understanding reached, or at least implied, in Jerusalem, the other two besides Paul who had been at the Jerusalem meeting—Peter and Barnabas—complied with the instructions from James. Judaism made provision for uncircumcised proselytes but not for completely nonobservant ones.[16]

It appears that Paul took advantage of the situation of the Diaspora where observance was comparatively lax and interpreted the Jerusalem agreement to include suspension of dietary laws. Paul's report shows that on his home ground, the Diaspora, he was willing to draw implications which would not have been acceptable in Jerusalem. In fairness to Paul, his contention was logical. In fairness to Peter, there is no indication that he finally agreed to Paul's demands. As the balance of Gal., ch. 2, shows, Paul's position was not based upon an agreement reached in Jerusalem but upon his own special doctrine of justification by faith which excluded observance of dietary laws. Certainly Jerusalem had not agreed to Paul's distinctive theology.

We must suppose that a personal issue was at stake for Paul to oppose Jerusalem so sharply. This was his apostleship. What Paul wanted most to demonstrate was his independence. This is the point of reporting his outburst against Peter. When not under this kind of pressure, Paul was wise enough, Jewish enough, to advise his converts to accommodate themselves to the consciences of the observant brethren in the church (Rom., chs. 14; 15).

James emerges from the sparse pre-Jamnia material about him as the effective head of the church both in Palestine and in the Diaspora. He enforced an observant Christian Judaism. Peter and Paul were both subject to that leadership, but the areas of their activity were divided. Peter was mainly responsible for the circumcised and Paul was to labor among the Gentiles (Gal. 2:7). This means that Peter's territory was Palestine, and Paul's was the Diaspora.[17] Both were equally concerned with Jews. Paul's ultimate allegiance to Jerusalem was symbolized in his agreement to gather money in the Diaspora for the brethren in Palestine (v. 10). During the lifetime of James, Christians were Jews.

It is impossible to date the book of James in the New Testament or to guess its author. We are dependent for the most part upon post-Jamnia literature for information about James and about the early church during the time of the separation of the church and Judaism. It will be necessary, therefore, to recognize in these sources the bitterness and prejudice this separation engendered.

The death of James is an event that is important to the story of the early church, even if only negative inferences can be drawn from it. Eusebius provides the Christian account of James's death from the *Hypotyposes* of Clement of Alexandria and from the *Memoirs* of Hegesippus. But these are as much in the style of the accounts of martyrdom that they have only legendary relation to the event. Eusebius uses the story to express the Christian view that the destruction of Jerusalem was a providential judgment upon the Jewish people. In this case, the Roman siege was the direct result of the execution of James. "At once Vespasian began to besiege them."[18] We can draw no conclusions from this account.[19]

Josephus gives a Jewish account of the death of James, not, however, without bias. The story in Josephus illustrates the cruelty of Sadducean judgments that outraged the sensibilities of the Pharisees and the public. The incident is necessary to Josephus' account since this execution was the occasion for the deposition of Annas from high-priestly office. Taking these functions of the story into account, the most we can conclude from Josephus is that James was a good Jew from a Pharisaic point of view and that his execution along with some others was not justified on grounds of breaking the law. This shows that the Christian Jews whom James represented were observant Jews and that the death of James was not evidence of their having been rejected by Judaism.

Josephus provides the date of the death by placing it between Festus and Albinus—A.D. 62. We may conclude then that, shortly before the rebellion against Rome, the Jerusalem church was an integral part of Judaism.[20] The next notice of the activity of the Jerusalem church was intended by its author to indicate that separation had begun.

This event is the flight of the Jerusalem church to Pella reported by Eusebius in connection with the rebellion against Rome that began in A.D. 66. The text is as follows:[21]

> The people of the church in Jerusalem were commanded by an oracle given by revelation before the war to those in the city who were worthy of it to depart and dwell in one of the cities of Perea which they called Pella. To it those who believe in Christ migrated from Jerusalem, that when holy men had altogether deserted the royal capital of the Jews and the whole land of Judea, the judgment of God might at last overtake them for all their crimes against the Christ and his Apostles, and all that generation of the wicked be utterly blotted out from among men.

This is obviously a climactic moment in Eusebius' historiography of vengeance. As such it assumes the complete separation of Christians from Jews. In Eusebius' mind, the providential function of the action of the Roman forces was to blot out all the non-Christian Jews of Judea, and, since Roman soldiers could not be expected to know the difference, Christian Jews had logically to be separated before the Romans came. There was precedent for Eusebius in Josephus' account of an oracular warning to Jews of the coming destruction. A certain Jesus, the son of Ananias, had predicted the destruction of the city throughout the four years preceding it.[22]

What is historically probable in Eusebius is that Christian Jews fled the city in A.D. 67 or 68 along with other Jewish moderates. Further, we have the famous account of the escape in a coffin by Johanan ben Zakkai, the founder of the Jamnia reconstruction, which indicates that many leading Pharisees must have left at the same time. Pharisees had generally followed a policy of peace with Rome, remembering the unfortunate experience in the Maccabean experiment. Christian Jews, who were Phariasaic in temperament anyway, would have had an additional reason for avoiding armed conflict. They believed that Jesus would return as the powerful Son of Man to do in the world what no human effort could accomplish. It was no mark against one's loyalty to Judaism to have escaped the destruction of the city.

It is, however, improbable that all Jewish Christians left the city. This conjecture simply reflects the vengeance motif in Eusebius' account. Nor is it probable that all Christian Jews went to Pella. There was no doubt that Christians had taken refuge in the church at Pella at the time of the destruction. Eusebius shows familiarity with the Pella tradition by his use of Ariston of Pella as a source for the story of the final destruction of Jerusalem under Hadrian. We know, also, that there were refugees already in Jamnia before Johanan ben Zakkai established the new center of Judaism there.[23] Eusebius had Christian Jews function as a single, distinct community since he had as much difficulty as many modern authors do in remembering that these refugees were after all Jews who would be at home wherever there were Jews.

Most Christian historians suppose that this was the end of the Jewish church. This ignores the evidence of its continued existence.

The destruction of Jerusalem was not the end of the Jewish church, but it was the beginning of very real difficulty for it. A church that hoped to convert people from Roman society would certainly find any identification with Judaism a handicap. There had been some occasions in the Hellenistic period when hostility to Jews found local expression. But the period of unrest in Palestine climaxed by the revolt of A.D. 66 was enough to convince the whole Roman world that Jews were a fanatical and incorrigible people. Palestinian Jews were subjected to all the suspicion and indignities of the conquered enemies of Rome and perhaps a third of the Jewish population in Palestine was destroyed.[24] Repercussions of the defeat were felt in Egypt where some Zealots fled to continue their opposition, resulting in the destruction of the temple of Onias at Leontopolis.[25] This flight to Egypt further confirmed the possibility for Christian Jews, like any other Jews, of escaping from Palestine into the Diaspora.

The customary victory parade was held in Rome to glorify Titus and humiliate the defeated Jews. The Arch of Titus in Rome shows sacred Temple furniture being carried in the triumphal procession. Thousands of Palestinian Jews were taken to Rome as slaves. The universal two-drachma tax for Jews on their temple was now levied on the temple of Jupiter Capitolinus. Judea was made an independent province whose wealth belonged to the emperor. The countryside was so ravaged by war and so much wealth was destroyed that priest and Sadducee disappeared, for Judea had been the source of their political and economic power. In summary, Judaism was deprived of its cultic center and any semblance of political autonomy. Its survival under the circumstances could only be attributed to its singular inner strength.

One of the most immediate effects of this embarrassment of Judaism in Rome was a new prominence for the nonobservant Gentile church. Paul's letters indicate that prior to this time the Gentile mission was peripheral to the main mission of the church which had been among the Jews. Paul had to fight for recognition of his mission. The central church at Jerusalem was an observant church under James; and Peter, the leader of the Twelve, was specifically responsible to the circumcised (Gal., ch. 2). The destruction of Jerusalem opened the way for a reversal of this order so that the originally secondary Gentile mission became primary.[26]

Granting this new primacy, the next step was to modify the Jewish origins of this Gentile mission in order to secure its future in Roman society. That is to say, having been established in this new position of prominence (by default, if you will) the survival of the Gentile church then depended upon making this originally Jewish faith more palatable to Roman culture.

Mark was the first New Testament book to attempt this modification of origins. He did it by his treatment of Jesus' ministry. We have already noticed how he changed the resurrection tradition into the translation of a Hellenistic Son of God. In the same story, the Judea that became infamous in the revolt was replaced by Galilee. We have also noted how Mark made Jesus antitemple by having him cleanse the Temple because it ought to be used by Gentiles for prayer rather than by Jews for sacrifice (Mark 11:17).

In keeping with this anticultic theme, Mark made Jesus the source of the freedom from the law enjoyed in the Gentile church. Mark carefully avoided any mention whatsoever of circumcision, for example; instead, he associated Christian faith with baptism which was relatively inoffensive to non-Jewish culture. And, what is more, Jesus was made to stand not for a continuance of the rite of water baptism but for a baptism of the Spirit which again would be more congenial to Roman culture (Mark 1:8). Sabbath observance, which was distinctly Jewish, was subjected to interpretation in the name of Jesus, the Son of Man (ch. 2:27). Jesus declared the laws of cleanness meaningless (ch. 7:19). He commended the substitution of the double commandment of love for the sacrificial system (ch. 12:33). When it appeared Jesus would observe the feast of the Passover (ch. 14:12, 14), he inaugurated instead a Hellenistic sacrament that disregarded the Jewish prohibition of blood (v. 24).

Mark was also sensitive to the revolutionary associations of Judaism that needed to be avoided. Contrary to the doctrine of the Zealots, Jesus found no conflict between the claims of Caesar and the claims of God (Mark 12:17). Mark was careful, in contrast to Matthew and Luke, to avoid a Jewish lineage for Jesus that would link him to the Davidic pretenders to a throne that opposed Roman sovereignty in Palestine. In fact, Mark had Jesus oppose any relationship between Messiahship and the insurrectionist Davidic line by countering this connection with a quotation from Psalm 110 (Mark 12:35–37). Jesus' repudiation of his family (ch. 3:33) would have the same effect. According to Eusebius, citing Hegesippus, Vespasian ordered the elimination of the family of David after the capture of Jerusalem.

This repudiation of family may also have been intended to serve another Marcan theme: the primacy of the mission to the Gentiles. When in Mark, Jesus taught that discipleship could mean separation from one's brother, Mark may have intended to eliminate James as an authority for the primacy of the Jewish mission. The other champion of the mission to the circumcised, Peter, was cast in the role of a misunderstanding leader of the disciples who ended by denying Jesus altogether. Having thus neutralized the traditional sponsors of the mission to the Jews, Mark then made the mission to the Gentiles a necessary prerequisite for the coming of the Son of Man (Mark 13:10). There is a marked advance here over Paul's understanding of the mission to the Gentiles. Paul had made the mission to the Gentiles a condition for the final salvation of the Jews (Rom. 11:25). Mark simply eliminated any special place for Jews by making the mission to the Gentiles the final opportunity for response to God's grace. In fact, he implied that Jewish failure to respond to the gospel had been destined by God (Mark 4:12).

Mark climaxed his separation of the church from its Jewish roots by the role he assigned the Jews of Jerusalem in the crucifixion of Jesus. Pilate, the Roman, recognized Jesus' innocence (Mark 15:14), and only agreed to crucify Jesus because of pressure from the Jewish crowd (v. 15). Jewish leaders were opposing Jesus out of sheer envy which Pilate, the Roman, perceived (v. 10). The hearing before the chief priests and council was intended to expose the injustice of Jewish legal proceedings and to provide grounds for ending the legal independence Judaism enjoyed under Rome. And finally Mark had the Palestinian Jews do exactly what Romans would expect who remembered the recent Jewish revolt. They preferred the release of Barabbas, a convicted rebel who had committed murder while participating in an insurrection, to Jesus, whose Kingship was patently nonpolitical. The centurion provided the final touch: although a Roman was responsible for succumbing to Jewish pressure to condemn an innocent man, he was compensated for by another Roman, the centurion, who was the only one in the Gospel, outside the demons, who really recognized Jesus for what he was, the Son of God (v. 39).

The scope of the present investigation precludes a more detailed exposition of Mark's cultural bias. This is enough perhaps to show that Mark represented the beginning of a massive attempt by the Gentile church to extricate Christianity from its Jewish origins in order to accommodate it to the Roman world. Meanwhile, Judaism was about the business of survival and in the process gave the church further reason to move in the direction Mark had already pioneered.

As we have already noted, the Christian Jews fled to Pella and other places in the Diaspora at the same time that other Jewish moderates were leaving Jerusalem. The most distinguished of these refugees was Rabban Johanan ben Zakkai, the founder of what became official Judaism. The accounts of his escape do not all agree.[27] They give essentially two versions. According to one account, he opposed the war altogether. He was known to be loyal and, upon escape, Vespasian offered him help; whereupon Johanan asked for permission to establish an academy in Jamnia. When this was granted, Johanan predicted Vespasian's elevation to emperor.[28] According to the second version, Johanan opposed the conduct of the war, favoring defensive action instead of the aggressiveness of the Zealots. When he met Vespasian he was unknown and had to justify himself. Then when he had made the flattering prediction of Vespasian's elevation and it had come to pass, Johanan was given permission to set up the academy in Jamnia.[29]

Although both accounts have legendary traits (Vespasian's election to emperor did not occur until a year later), the second is more legendary and is obviously later. It also showed interest in protecting Johanan from the reputation of having been a defector. In the first account, the loyalist sympathies of Johanan provided the ground for permission to go to Jamnia.

This is historically more probable than Vespasian's agreeing to Johanan's request because Johanan was such an impressive prophet. Then Johanan ben Zakkai was granted amnesty because Rome banked on his kind of Pharisee to be the new foundation of a Palestinian Judaism that could reconcile itself to existence under the regency of Rome. Rome's faith in Johanan was well placed because he lent his considerable powers to the elimination of all competing kinds of Judaism. And Judaism's survival of this revolt and of the one under Bar-Cochba is a tribute to his wisdom. The circumstances of Johanan's escape point to the spring of A.D. 68.[30]

The situation was fantastically difficult for anyone who wished to begin to reconstitute legitimate Jewish authority. In Jamnia there was the atmosphere of bitterness and defeat even before Jerusalem fell. Some of the last acts of official Judaism in Jerusalem had been to sever all connections between Jews and Gentiles. When Johanan arrived there, Jamnia had already been subdued by these very Gentiles and resettled with loyalist refugees.[31] When Jerusalem fell, and with it the Temple, Jews were bound to wonder whether they had been rejected by God and their religion destroyed. They reacted with despair and an intensified longing for a utopian solution to their problems in some realm beyond history.

The situation required decisive action. The way Johanan symbolized the transfer of authority from Jerusalem to Jamnia illustrated his ability to operate where no precedent existed to guide him. According to tradition, when New Year fell on a Sabbath the shofar could only be blown in the Temple of Jerusalem and it could not be blown anywhere else. The Talmud shows how Johanan dealt with this occasion.

Our Rabbis taught: Once New Year fell on a Sabbath [and all the towns assembled], and Rabban Johanan said to the Bene Bothgra, Let us blow the *shofar*. They said to him, Let us discuss the matter. He said to them, Let us blow and afterwards discuss. After they had blown they said to

him, Let us now discuss the question. He replied: The
horn has already been heard in Jabneh, and what has been
done is no longer open to discussion.[32]

The effect was to claim for Jamnia, and eventually for all rabbinical courts, the authority of the Temple and the Sanhedrin.[33]
Johanan carried out the displacing of the Temple with a series
of enactments that either suspended ritual and liturgy that depended on the Temple or provided for their continuance until
the Temple might be rebuilt.

This amounted to an elimination of the influence of one
group in Israel that had competed with Pharisees for dom-
inance in Judaism—the priests. Replacement of the Temple by
the rabbinical court also meant replacement of former Temple
officials, of course. In particular, the president of the court assumed the authority which had traditionally belonged to the
high priest. The president, or Nasi, was now in a position from
which he could attempt to make his brand of Judaism normative not only in Palestine but in the Diaspora as well.

What was needed now was a definite substitution of some
aspects of Pharisaic piety for what the Temple had provided.
Johanan also offered this. When Rabbi Joshua lamented the
ruined Temple because with it had disappeared the means of
atoning for Israel's iniquities, Johanan replied: "We have another atonement as effective as this. . . . It is acts of loving
kindness, as it is said, *For I desire mercy* and not sacrifice"
(Hos. 6:6).[34]

But the priestly party was not the only competition. To neu-
tralize the widespread expectation of an apocalyptic solution
to Judaism's problems, Johanan tried to maintain a balance
with the requirements of ongoing common life. "If you have
a sapling in your hand, and it is said to you, Behold there is
the Messiah, go on with your planting and afterward go out
and receive him."[35]

The greatest threat to Johanan came of course from the Zealots. Johanan was himself convinced that peace was the only

way but, as the next revolt would show sixty years later, Judaism was not yet completely convinced. Zealotism was still vigorous enough in Johanan's day for Zealot refugees from Palestine to cause disturbances in Egypt at Alexandria and Cyrene.

With the disappearance of the Temple and Sanhedrin, the Sadducees lost the basis for their influence upon Judaism. The Essenes suffered a similar fate. The remains of the destruction of the Essene community at Qumran and the absence of records of subsequent Essene influence lead to the conclusion that this party had come to its end with the rise of Jamnian Judaism. One other aberration had still to be singled out and eliminated: Christian Judaism. This was done under Johanan's successor, Gamaliel II.

Not only did Johanan put Pharisaism well on its way to becoming the dominant expression of Judaism, he also gave the Pharisaic sage a new status in Israel. He inaugurated the ordination of his disciples into the office of rabbi. This made "rabbi" an official title and gave the sage for the first time a place in the polity of Judaism.[36]

Johanan had the personal gifts and the initiative to pioneer the new direction, but Gamaliel II had better credentials for continuing leadership that could develop broader support for Jamnia throughout Judaism. Gamaliel had remained in Jerusalem until the end of the fighting so that he was not liable to the suspicion of being a Roman sympathizer while Jerusalem was still fighting for its life. Gamaliel was also further qualified as heir to the prestige of the house of Hillel and of the family of David.[37] There is no information about the transfer of leadership from Johanan to Gamaliel, except that it happened while Johanan was alive. He continued his own career at Beror Heil in opposition to Gamaliel.[38] The transfer probably took place after the end of fighting in A.D. 73.

Gamaliel carried out his program with greater consistency and success than had Johanan. The objectives of his program were to establish unity by curbing dispute and individual practice.[39] He was so determined in the elimination of variant opinions that the sages revolted and deposed him from the presidency until the practice was established of including individual opinions in the tradition and especially of recording the minority opinion in a case. Gamaliel was so determined to eliminate dissent that he did not hesitate to excommunicate his brother-in-law, Rabbi Eliezer. In such an atmosphere it was perhaps inevitable, though nonetheless tragic, that Christian Jews would be banned.

As a Galilean movement, the Christian Jews were already suspect by the sages. According to tradition, Johanan had lived in Galilee sometime between A.D. 20 and 40 for eighteen years.[40] His final impression after having had only two cases referred to him during his whole sojourn was, "O Galilee, Galilee! Thou hatest the Torah!"[41] Johanan deplored the Galilean lack of learning as over and against Galilean enthusiasm. Christian Jews could hardly escape association with the Zealot movement which had been Galilean. The continued apocalyptic expectation of the Christian Jews only confirmed the suspicion of instability that arose from their Galilean associations. The primary attention of Jamnia, however, focused upon the nonobservant, apparently anti-Pharisaic, wing of the church in the Diaspora. This direction must have seemed especially insidious to the leaders of Jamnia since it, in effect, reinforced the natural tendency of the Diaspora toward laxity—all in the name of a truer Palestinian Judaism.

We have already noted Johanan's skepticism toward popular messianic movements. The church's claim that the Messiah had come and would come again soon could only complicate relations with Rome when Judaism was seeking to relieve itself of association with revolution. The same political concern which probably led to the crucifixion of Jesus would continue at Jamnia to provide reason to avoid his followers.

The specific measure Gamaliel took to exclude Christian Judaism from emerging normative Judaism was so drastic that it betrays what a formidable force Christian Judaism had become. It, along with Zealotism, was probably Pharisaism's chief competitor. To tie Judaism together by worship, Gamaliel arranged the order of the Prayer of Eighteen Petitions and made it obligatory upon all Jews in private daily devotion.[42] It was also a regular part of the liturgy of the synagogue. This common liturgical thread binding all Judaism together became the medium for the ban against Christian Judaism. The ban became petition number twelve. Its oldest known form is: "For apostates may there be no hope, and may the Nazarenes and heretics (*minim*) suddenly perish."[43] The benediction takes its name from the word for heretic (*min*)—*Birkat Haminim*. It was composed by Samuel the Little for Gamaliel.[44] Samuel died about a decade after the destruction of the Temple.[45] This dates the *birkat* in the late seventies or early eighties when we must assume the enmity between Jamnia Jews and Jews with Christian convictions came to a climax.

There is little doubt that the Benediction as Gamaliel took it from Samuel was directed especially against Christian Jews, although there was an earlier form with another target.[46] The Jamnia Benediction was designed to root Christian Jews out of the synagogue where we must suppose they were at home until this time. During worship, a suspected Christian Jew could be asked to lead the prayer. If he would not include the twelfth benediction, he revealed himself as a *min* and was removed. In order that it might function effectively as a test, this was the only benediction among the eighteen that had to be recited exactly according to the prescribed text.[47] It would be difficult to overexaggerate the import of this step against Christian Judaism. First it proves that Christian Judaism was an important force within Judaism. Secondly, it shows that Christian Jews were to be deprived of their spiritual and cultural home. One must expect a bitterness to develop within the emerging new religion.

This enactment of Jamnia was not intended only for Palestine. Once the decision had been made, the new posture toward Christians was undoubtedly communicated immediately throughout the Diaspora for universal Jewish enforcement.

From now on there could be no important community of Jews anywhere in the world in which the Christian message could be heard in a neutral atmosphere as Luke says was once the case in Rome (Acts 28:21).

The president of the academy at Jamnia had apostles at his disposal precisely for the purpose of communicating the judgments of the court to the Diaspora and to help enforce the decrees as well as to report whether they were being obeyed. This apostolic system of communication was necessary to the publication of the annual calendar upon which observance the festivals depended. It was also necessary to maintain the presidency since on their missions the apostles collected a tax imposed for the support of the president.

Acts 28:21 has the leader of the Jews in Rome mention letters from Judea which might have given information about Paul. This accurately reflects later practice under Jamnia. Rabbinic sources contain mention of the letters from Gamaliel to Jews in the Diaspora which announced the adjustment of the calendar by a thirteenth month[48] as well as other letters to the Diaspora from Simeon ben Gamaliel and Johanan ben Zakkai.[49] Eusebius also recorded delivery of such letters.[50]

The letters of most interest to our study are ones that announced the exclusion of Christians from Judaism by means of the special "Benediction Against Heretics." It would be natural for Gamaliel to dispatch letters on this subject to the Diaspora immediately upon the official adoption of this benediction.[51] We have what is most probably a description of just these letters in the writings of Justin, Eusebius, and Jerome.[52] According to Justin these letters were carried by Jamnian apostles. The connection of the letters with the "Benediction Against Heretics" is established by the allusion to the cursing of Christians.[53]

It is possible to reconstruct what was probably a summary of their contents from Justin, although he is admittedly a prejudiced witness. In the nature of the case, no other kind is available. Of all the teachings of Christians the resurrection of Jesus seems to have received most attention. In rebuttal of the church's claim Jamnia accused the disciples of stealing the body in order to support the fraud of his resurrection. The rest of the polemic was aimed at the lawless teaching of Jesus and at the church's claim he was Messiah, a teacher from God, and the Son of God. All witnesses agree the letters had wide distribution.

This attack upon Christians represented a new epoch in the relations between Judaism and Jews with Christian convictions. Before Jamnia, the controversy seemed to be primarily and almost solely over the observance of the law. The Christian convictions that Jesus was the Messiah and had risen from the dead seemed to have been permissible within Judaism. Heavenly visions and eschatological convictions about various figures who commanded a following were common within Judaism. Only after the destruction of Jerusalem, when Judaism was fighting for its very existence, did those convictions become dangerous heresies that threatened the existence of the parent religious community. Luke's report of the advice of Gamaliel I is an accurate reflection of the permissive attitude possible before the destruction. "Keep away from these men and let them alone; for if this plan or this undertaking is of men, it will fail; but if it is of God, you will not be able to overthrow them. You might even be found opposing God!" (Acts 5:38–39.) The problem of survival did not permit the sages at Jamnia to be so tolerant.

This direct attack upon the central doctrines of primitive Christianity must reflect the influence of nonobservant Christians among Jews of the Diaspora after the destruction. Any drift away from the law had to be opposed, for Pharisaism was convinced that only by unqualified respect for law could Judaism survive.

Nonobservant Christianity was busy qualifying just this respect for law. This was being done in the name of Jesus the risen Messiah and Son of God. His teaching was being used to determine the will of God instead of Pharisaic tradition. Since

Jesus was being used as the foundation for a non-Pharisaic attitude toward law, the person of Jesus must now be attacked. This was a new element in the conversation between Jews with Christian convictions and other Jews.

Other reactions to Christian teaching confirm the atmosphere of radical rejection. The Talmud explained later that the first-century prohibition against fasting on Sunday was to prevent the appearance that Jews might be observing the day Christians set apart to mark the resurrection of Jesus.[54] The rift with Christians affected the attitude toward proselytizing. Judaism had been active and effective in this. However, Eliezer ben Hyrcanus, a pupil of Johanan ben Zakkai, began a tradition of opposition to converts.[55] This was connected with the fact that Christian converts no doubt came largely from the proselytes on the fringes of the synagogue. Gamaliel II's denial that children of Gentiles had any place in the world to come[56] belonged to the same pattern of reaction. Jamnia's program to eliminate Christians and other dissenters was no doubt advanced by Gamaliel's tour of the Diaspora on his visit to Rome in 95.[57] While there he definitely argued against Christians who interpreted Hos. 5:6 as the rejection of Israel by the God of Israel.[58]

The effect of this separation of the two religious communities was not only to purify Jamnian Judaism of a powerful dissenting movement but also to expose Christians before Rome as atheists without a legal standing for their religion.

Christians reacted sharply to the rejection by Judaism. It reinforced the direction we have seen nonobservant Christians were already taking and accommodated Christianity to Roman culture. Matthew and Luke each in his own way reflected the church's reaction to this rejection by Judaism.

Matthew's passion narrative showed a new bitterness toward Judaism. Whereas Mark portrayed the Jews as jealous revolutionaries, Matthew charged them with full awareness of the crime of crucifying the Messiah. The consequence of this crime in Matthew was the perpetual guilt of the Jews. Matthew had all the Jews in attendance upon the crucifixion respond, "His blood be on us and on our children!" (Matt. 27:25). It was the "children"—the Jews who were the author's contemporaries—who were the main concern of this Gospel. The author of Matthew wished to establish the guilt of the Jews who were his contemporaries and not merely the guilt of the generation in which the crucifixion took place.

A comparison of Matthew's resurrection story with the content of the letters against Christians issued at Jamnia confirmed the anti-Jamnia setting of this Gospel. The letters against Christians issued by Gamaliel II contained the same polemic against the resurrection which Matthew undertook to answer by his modification of Mark's empty tomb story. Mark showed no awareness of the vulnerability of his story. The implication was that this polemic developed at Jamnia in response to the new form of resurrection invented by Mark, and that Matthew wrote, at least in part, to counter the attacks of Jamnia. If Matthew came from Antioch or some similar center of Jewish culture, his Christian Jewish community may well have learned of this counter to the empty tomb story in the letters of Gamaliel II from Jamnia. Matthew revealed in a side comment that the Jewish answer to the empty tomb was being propagated in his own time. "This story has been spread among the Jews to this day." (Matt. 28:15.) This is an apt description of the publication from Jamnia of the official Jewish rebuttal.

The Sermon on the Mount also illustrated the Jamnia setting of Matthew.[59] The "massive elevation of the teaching of Jesus" in the Sermon and the desire to define a new way for a community that was emerging as the new Israel to parallel the way the rabbis were defining the way at Jamnia for old Israel are best explained by juxtaposition with Jamnia. The parallels between the Lord's Prayer and the Shemoneh Esreh provide a striking illustration of the point.[60]

Matthew 23:5–10 probably reflected Matthew's reaction to Jamnia's elevation of "rabbi" to a title for officially ordained sages.[61] Prior to the creation of ordination at Jamnia, a rabbi had no official status in Judaism. Now "rabbi" became a mark of educational achievement and community status.

This passage introduced the bitter invective against the "scribes and Pharisees" that was the most startling feature of this Gospel. The tirade culminated in fixing guilt for the death of all righteous Jews who were rejected by other Jews upon the current generation. This is the same bloodguilt we had already noticed in the passion narrative. The intensity of the bitterness and its exclusive direction against "scribes and Pharisees" can best be accounted for as the reaction of Christian Jews who had been banned from Judaism by the Pharisaic leaders of Jamnia. The persecution mentioned in vs. 34 and 35 probably reflected the rejection of Matthew's community that resulted from the ban.

We have noted the evidence for a change of attitude at Jamnia toward proselytizing and the complementary doctrine that Gentiles have a place in the world to come. Matthew could hardly take a more contrary view than the one he expressed in his final pericope. He had the risen Lord declare that the main function of the church was to go to the Gentiles, just when official Judaism was rejecting all conversation with the non-Jewish world.[62] Matthew had prepared the way for this move toward the Gentiles by having Jesus predict that the Kingdom would be taken away from the Jews who rejected Jesus and "given to a nation producing the fruits of it" (Matt. 21:43).[63]

The reaction of Matthew's community to the measures being taken at Jamnia of course contributed to the great schism. But Matthew was no doubt unaware that he was founding what was to become another religion, a third race, an alternative to Judaism. He and his community were convinced that the right future of Israel lay in their direction. They felt that they were the true Jews. This accounts for the apparent ambiguity in Matthew's attitude toward Judaism. He accepted the heritage of Judaism but disputed the direction it was officially taking. Respect for heritage is illustrated by his recognition of the

authority of "Moses' seat" (Matt. 23:2) and in his insistence
that the Sermon on the Mount was a fulfillment of law and not
another law (ch. 5:17, 20). His insistence on another direction
was just as evident in his rejection of the Pharisaic understanding of heritage at each decisive point. No doubt the direction
Matthew's community was taking was newer than they themselves knew or could admit. This is nowhere more obvious than
in Matthew's acceptance of the Son of God Christology and of
the sacramentalism of the nonobservant church. When such
religious symbols became decisive for his community, Matthew
was well on his way to offering an option that was impossible
for a Judaism that was in the process of rejecting all Gentile
culture. By adopting the position of the Gentile church in
Christology and sacrament, Matthew was just as effectively, if
unwittingly, eliminating space for a consistently Jewish Christian. In so doing, he documented the beginning of the transition
from Judaism to Christianity. It will now become possible to
speak of Christianity as an entity distinct from Judaism. This
would have been a startling innovation for both Matthew and
Paul.

It is a tribute to Luke's originality that he went on to make
this conceptually possible while still claiming a Jewish heritage
for Christianity. The definitive work of Conzelmann has made
this theological achievement of Luke a familiar story. What is
not so familiar is the evidence in Luke's work for the persistence
of Christian Judaism. It is commonly assumed that Christian
Judaism promptly atrophied and withered away when rejected
both by its parent community and by its only possible alternate
sponsor, Gentile Christianity. To see that this was not the case
will help to establish the original vigor and continuing importance of Christian Judaism after A.D. 70, in spite of the prevailing prejudice against the idea of a continuing important Jewish
Christian community.

Luke cannot be adequately understood and evaluated apart
from an appreciation of his particular historical setting. His
most probable date is around A.D. 90 to 100, but one attempt to

date Luke put him as late as the middle of the second century.[64] This date was based upon a comparison of Luke with Justin Martyr. This attempt did *not* establish that they were contemporaries. The comparison did show that Luke shared an anti-Jewish bias with the church fathers of the second quarter of the second century.[65] This comparison helps us appreciate how far from Judaism Luke's church had traveled.

Toward the middle of the second century the church had become conscious of itself as the ordained replacement for Judaism.[66] In fact, it contended, Judaism had had little real place in God's plan except as a foil for the supplanting role of the church. According to Justin (who died about A.D. 165) there never had been a Christian Jewish church in the sense that Christianity had been merely a party within Judaism. The church of his time claimed the Jews rejected the gospel from the beginning and, following this rejection, God's grace and purpose passed to the Gentile church. The Old Testament predicted all this, but only the church was capable of the correct interpretation. This proved that the Old Testament belonged to the church and not to Jews who could not understand it.

Luke reflects a similar attitude toward Judaism in his treatment of the roles of James, Peter, and Paul in Acts. James barely appeared except to legitimize Paul's mission. What became of him and the Christian Jewish Palestinian church is unimportant. Peter was freed from association with that church and became the first apostle to the Gentiles. This was in order to introduce the main story of God's action by the Spirit in the missionary career of Paul. The geographical movement was symbolic of God's favor. The gospel was finally for Rome, not Palestine. The climax was Paul's speech to the Jews in Rome (Acts 28:25–28). Isaiah predicted their unbelief. Only one course was left open to Paul: the symbol of the true mission of the church. "Let it be known to you then that this salvation of God has been sent to the Gentiles; they will listen." (V. 28.)

The anti-Jewish bias is manifest. Actually James had led the whole church in his day. Peter was probably one of his lieutenants. Paul and the Gentile church were a subordinate dissenting element who never did achieve full acceptance by the mother church in Jerusalem. Peter was primarily related to the circumcised and not the uncircumcised, as we learned from Galatians. Luke's bias against Jewish Christians helps document the fact that his church was as separated from Judaism as was the church of the fathers. On the other hand, Luke also showed that there were still Jewish Christians in his church who had to be taken into account. Luke's Gentile church made concessions over sacraments, law, and Christology for the sake of these Christian Jews. These concessions to a Jewish point of view are the evidence for the continued vigor of Christian Judaism within the very movement that purposed to eliminate it. Given Luke's probable dating, this points to Jewish Christians who were still strong in the Western church toward the end of the first century.[67]

Although the Jewish Christians in Luke's church attended the celebration of the Lord's Supper, they could not accept the theological implications of the form we encountered in Mark, Matthew, and Paul. These forms demanded the interpretation of Jesus' death as the institution of a new covenant implying, of course, that the old covenant was defective and obsolete. This would be equivalent to a denial of the finality of the original covenant and of the validity of the Jewish religion. Christians who considered themselves primarily Jews could not lend their support to this belittling of their native convictions. For their sake, most probably, Luke eliminated the symbol of a cup of blood with its accompanying mention of another covenant. Instead the cup became an occasion for hope of reunion in the future Kingdom of God—a hope all Jews could share.

Luke put the cup before the bread, reversing the traditional order in the Gentile church. This was an accommodation to Jewish custom because, according to Marcan and Matthean accounts, the Lord's Supper resulted from Jesus' desire to celebrate Passover (Mark 14: 12–16; Matt. 26: 17–19). Then each substituted a Hellenistic sacrament instead. Only Luke, presumably under pressure of a Jewish group in his church, carried this Passover context into the Supper story: "I have earnestly desired to eat this passover with you before I suffer" (Luke 22:15). The cup came first because the cup initiated the Passover liturgy.[68] The bread assumed the function we have observed in the Emmaus story. It was the sacramental means by which the risen Lord was bodily present. Both cup and bread in this order with these meanings attached could very well accompany a Passover celebration without intruding a substitute redemption based on the death of Jesus as do the forms of Mark, Matthew, and Paul. Hans Lietzmann showed that there was a Jewish Christian community that celebrated both the Lord's Supper and Passover.[69] This helps to confirm our explanation of Luke.

Luke did not include in his account of the Lord's Supper the saying that the cup of wine is the blood of the new covenant. This form of the supper was partially a result of the agreement reached at the Jerusalem Council not to partake of blood (Acts 15:29). (The restrictions placed upon the Gentile converts by that council approximated in part the Noachian law presumably binding on God-fearers.[70]) Luke had Paul agree to this decision of the Jerusalem Council, but Paul's report in Galatians of his settlement with Jerusalem cannot be reconciled with Luke's report of that settlement in Acts, ch. 15.[71] Most probably what Paul actually agreed to was a collection for the poor in Jerusalem. It would have been against the basic principle of his gospel to accept the legal restrictions recorded in Acts, ch. 15.

The conflict between Luke's account in Acts and Paul's account in Galatians disappears if the real setting for Luke is after the separation of Judaism and Christianity.[72] Luke's church was making place for what must have been a horde of Christian Jews seeking a home in the Gentile church as a result of being ousted from synagogue fellowship. It follows that "the party of the Pharisees" (Acts 15:5) who demanded circumcision and observance of the whole law of Moses were not James's contemporaries but the dominant party in the new normative Judaism being formulated at Jamnia. Luke's church judged that their demand was unreasonable but accepted a compromise with Christian Jews to the effect that Gentile brethren should observe some minimal law. In some such fashion as Acts, ch. 15, which may indeed reflect an early tradition,[73] the postseparation church found a way for its two cultural wings to live together in mutual acceptance. The form of the pronouncement of the Council betrayed the relation to the new Judaism of Jamnia. The letter to Gentile brethren in Antioch, Syria, and Cilicia was modeled on letters being issued to the Diaspora by the court of Jamnia. The force of this Jewish Christian inspired concession was felt throughout the second century. Justin, Eusebius, and Tertullian testify to the continuing Christian aversion to blood.[74]

Christology is the third area in which Luke revealed the presence of Christian Jews in his community. But since the Christian Jewish view of Jesus is the subject of the next chapter, we reserve Luke's treatment of Christology until then. There is, however, one other indication that Luke was accommodating to Christian Jews in the church. This indication is in the passion narrative.

We have already observed how Mark diverted the blame for the crucifixion away from Pilate toward jealous insurrectionist "Jews." Matthew, we have seen, went farther and fixed the bloodguilt for the crucifixion not only upon Jews who were Jesus' contemporaries but also upon their children; that is, upon the Jews who were Matthew's opponents. Luke undertook to reverse this blame-laying tendency. He did so by means of his motif of ignorance. Only in Luke's account does Jesus say from the cross, "Father, forgive them; for they know not what they do" (Luke 23:34). Luke carried the same motif into the apostolic preaching. In the scene where Peter healed the lame man at the Temple gate, Luke with one stroke obliterated the vengeance which the church before him had been accumulating against Judaism. He had Peter say: "And now, brethren, I know that you acted in ignorance, as did also your rulers. But what God foretold by the mouth of all the prophets, that his Christ should suffer, he thus fulfilled" (Acts 3:17–18). Luke replaced vengeance with divine necessity. Accordingly, Luke softened the hostility of the crowd at the crucifixion in Mark and Matthew by the lament before the crucifixion and after the death (Luke 23: 27, 48). Luke took pains to prevent the crucifixion from alienating Christian Jews from his community.

It has been generally recognized that Luke was the beginning of "catholic" theology.[75] J. C. O'Neill contributed to the discussion by attempting to pinpoint Luke in the development of the church's thought by his affinity to Justin Martyr. What he and others have failed to appreciate is that Luke's attitude toward Christian Jews reflected their presence in his church. The evidence in Luke of the continued vigor of Jewish Christianity in the West is overlooked because Luke so subtly assimilated them into his early catholicism.

Luke is not the only evidence for Christian Jews after the great divorce. The Bar-Cochba revolt gave a new impetus to Judaism's opposition to Christians in their midst. The revolt was itself, at least partially, a reaction to Christianity. Contrary to all its historical experience with armed revolt, Pharisaism committed itself to a military messiah. When it did so, one must suppose it was partly to counter Christianity's claim to have the Messiah. The bitterness against Christian Jews led Bar-Cochba to execute those who would not renounce Jesus as the Messiah.[76] This following upon the ban of the "Benediction Against Heretics," finally alienated Christian Jews. Only now did they cease to be a distinct wing of the church.

According to Eusebius' list of bishops, the leadership of the Jerusalem church now passed from bishops of the circumcision to bishops of the uncircumcision.[77] This list was created about A.D. 200 but goes back to a list of Hegesippus from about the year 150. In Hegesippus, we find a probable illustration of the kind of Christian with Jewish heritage for whose sake the

Lucan compromise was devised. Eastern Jewish Christians, such as Hegesippus, were so satisfied by the arrangement that they were not only at home in the Western "catholic" church of the second century but contributed significantly to the effort to establish it as the standard of orthodoxy.

The figure of Hegesippus is somewhat obscured by the smoke of scholarly conflict. He is certainly not the hero of a militant Judaizing party, as the Tübingen school wished to believe. On the other hand, it is unfair to deny any connection with a Jewish heritage.[78] Eusebius provides adequate grounds for his inference that Hegesippus was a convert "from among the Hebrews." Hegesippus had quoted the gospel according to the Hebrews, showed knowledge of Syriac and Aramaic, and cited Jewish oral tradition.[79] In his respect for James and the Jewish bishops of Jerusalem, Hegesippus showed those sympathies to which Luke accommodated himself. An obvious veneration of James inspired Hegesippus' account of James's martyrdom.[80] Hegesippus showed similar respect for Symeon, the successor of James as bishop of Jerusalem, in the account of his death.[81] In the same connection, Hegesippus also reported the fate of relatives of Jesus who led churches until the death of Simon, the son of Clopas. In fact, according to Hegesippus, the virginal purity of the Jerusalem church continued only so long as the descendants of Jesus led that church.[82]

In tracing the line of bishops at Jerusalem, Hegesippus represents the view of the primacy of the Christian Jewish church in Jerusalem which Luke made the keystone of his account of the early church. Recently, new evidence has been discovered of a continuing Jewish Christian church.[83] We shall have occasion to look at it in the next chapter.

It is not necessary to carry the story of the growth of hostility between Judaism and its new competitor any farther. Enough has been told to show that Jewish culture could not be the way of the church's future in a predominantly Greco-Roman or Hellenistic cultural situation. Therefore, when the church formulated the career of Jesus, this career was adapted to

Hellenistic cultural needs and Jesus' Jewishness was minimized.

One could say that the first quest of the historical Jesus was biased in favor of Hellenistic culture and against Jewish culture. But once this cultural bias has been exposed, there is a chance that when we follow the second generation's way from heavenly resurrection to earthly career we need not perpetuate this bias against Jesus' native culture. We are freed to some extent to encounter a Jesus who is more Jewish than the ex-Jewish church could afford to tolerate. And in the process, we shall find a Jesus who not only was more firmly at home in this world but also one whose culture is more in tune with the modern world than the traditional figure apparently alienated from his own people.

NOTES

1. Neill Hamilton, "Temple Cleansing and Temple Bank," *Journal of Biblical Literature,* Vol. 83 (1964), pp. 365 ff.

2. Cf. Oscar Cullmann, *The State in the New Testament* (Charles Scribner's Sons, 1956), pp. 41–43.

3. M. Hengel, *Die Zeloten* (Leiden/Köln, 1961), pp. 57, 58, 96, 385–386; Emil Schürer, *A History of the Jewish People in the Time of Jesus* (Schocken Books, Inc., 1961), p. 197.

4. Cullmann, *op. cit.,* pp. 11–17.

5. *Ibid.,* p. 14.

6. Hans Lietzmann, *An die Korinther, I, II,* 4th enlarged ed. by Werner G. Kümmel (Tübingen, 1949), p. 150; Hans Windisch, *Der zweite Korintherbrief* (Göttingen, 1924), p. 356.

7. An uncircumcised convert to Judaism was possible, cf. H. J. Schoeps, *Paul: The Theology of the Apostle in the Light of Jewish Religious History,* tr. by Harold Knight (The Westminster Press, 1961), p. 66.

8. These were, for example, the Gnostics whom we met in the discussion of resurrection (I Cor., ch. 15). They missed the necessity of a body since they were lacking a Jewish appreciation of history. Paul answers with an argument for history expressed in the form of an argument for a bodily resurrection.

9. The so-called acute Hellenization of Christianity is post-Pauline (Schoeps, *op. cit.*, p. 48).

10. An epitome of this author reminds us of Paul: "[He] despairs of a life of absolute obedience to the Law. . . . The unconscious and unexpressed cry of the book is for a moral dynamic which legalism could not supply" (R. H. Charles, *The Apocrypha and Pseudepigrapha of the Old Testament* [London: Oxford University Press, 1913], Vol. II, p. 557).

11. Schoeps's appreciation of Paul's dilemma in dealing with this new eschatological situation is magnificent. "The eschatology of Paul . . . is distinguished from all forms of Jewish speculation by the fact that in consequence of the resurrection of Jesus from the dead it considers the eschaton to have already begun." (P. 98.) He misses, however, the root of Paul's Son of God Christology when he attributes it to Jesus instead of the resurrection as Paul clearly does (Rom. 1:4) (*op. cit.*, pp. 150, 158).

12. Josephus, *Antiquities* iv. 326.

13. Philo, *De Posteritate Caini* 28 ff.; *De Vita Mosis* II. 2 ff., 288 ff.; Hans Windisch, *Paulus und Christus* (Leipzig, 1931), p. 106; Erwin R. Goodenough, *By Light Light: The Mystic Gospel of Hellenistic Judaism* (Yale University Press, 1935), p. 128; Erwin R. Goodenough, *An Introduction to Philo Judaeus* (Barnes & Noble, Inc., 1962), pp. 145–152; Schoeps, *op. cit.*, pp. 32, 33, 156, 157.

14. Schoeps, *op. cit.*, pp. 151–157.

15. Gerhard Kittel, art. *"apostolos," Theologisches Wörterbuch zum Neuen Testament*, I, pp. 416–417; Hans von Campenhausen, *Kirchliches Amt und geistliche Vollmacht in den ersten drei Jahrhunderten* (Tübingen, 1953), pp. 23 ff.

16. Schoeps, *op. cit.*, p. 66. But Schoeps mistakenly credits Luke over against Paul in spite of the recognition that the predominant tendency of Luke is "to conceal by its mode of presentation the inner divisions of the apostolic age" (p. 69).

17. E. Burton, *The Epistle to the Galatians* (Edinburgh, 1921), pp. 97, 98; Heinrich Schlier, *Der Brief an die Galater* (Göttingen, 1951), p. 46.

18. Eusebius, *Historia Ecclesiastica* II. 23, 21–24 (Loeb).

19. Maurice Goguel, *The Birth of Christianity* (Humanities Press, Inc., 1953), pp. 127 ff.

20. S. G. F. Brandon, *The Fall of Jerusalem and the Christian Church* (London: S.P.C.K., 1957), p. 100.

21. Eusebius, *Historia Ecclesiastica* III. 4, 31.

22. *Ibid.*, III. i, 7–9.

23. Josephus, *War* iv. 3:2 (130), 8:1 (444).

24. *Ibid.*, vi. 9:3 (420–430); Judah Goldin, "The Period of the Talmud," *The Jews: Their History, Culture, and Religion,* ed. by Louis Finkelstein, 2d ed. (Harper & Brothers, 1955), Vol. I, p. 144, n. 12.

25. Josephus, *War* vi. 10–11.

26. J. C. O'Neill, *The Theology of Acts in Its Historical Setting* (London: S.P.C.K., 1961), pp. 104–105.

27. *Avot de Rabbi Natan* a, Ch. 4, ed. by Solomon Schechter (New York, 1945), tr. by Judah Goldin (Yale University Press, 1955); *Avot de Rabbi Natan* b, Ch. 6, *Lamentations Rabba* to vs. 1:31; *Babylonian Talmud,* 56, a–b.

28. *Avot de Rabbi Natan.*

29. *Lamentations Rabba.*

30. Jacob Neusner, *A Life of Rabban Johanan ben Zakkai* (Leiden, 1962), p. 113.

31. Josephus, *War* iv. 3:2 and 8:1.

32. *Babylonian Talmud,* Rosh Hashanah 29b, tr. by Maurice Simon, Soncino ed. (London, 1938).

33. *Mishnah* Rosh Hashanah 4:1.

34. *The Fathers According to Rabbi Nathan,* tr. by Judah Goldin (Yale University Press, 1955), Ch. 4, p. 34.

35. Schechter, *Avot de Rabbi Natan,* Ch. 34a.

36. Neusner, *op. cit.,* p. 167.

37. *Ibid.,* p. 167.

38. *Babylonian Talmud,* Sanhedrin, 32b.

39. Goldin, *loc. cit.,* p. 150.

40. Neusner, *op. cit.,* pp. 27–28.

41. *Ibid.,* p. 29. S. W. Baron, *A Social and Religious History*

of the Jews, 2d rev. ed. (Columbia University Press, 1952), Vol. I, p. 279; *Palestinian Talmud* 16:9.

42. *Babylonian Talmud*, Megillah 176, Berakot 286, end; *Misnah* Berakot 4:3.

43. George F. Moore, *Judaism in the First Centuries of the Christian Era, the Age of the Tannain* (Harvard University Press, 1954), Vol. I, p. 292, n. 8. Cf. Louis Finkelstein, "The Development of the Amidah," *Jewish Quarterly Review*, Vol. XVI, No. 2, p. 156.

44. *Babylonian Talmud*, Berakot 286.

45. *Babylonian Talmud*, Sotah 486, Soncino Edition, n. 9. This passage honors Samuel of whom a *Bath Kol* said he was worthy to receive the *Shechinah*. *Tosefta* Sotah 13, 3f has "holy spirit" for Shechinah.

46. Baron, *op cit.*, Vol. II, p. 135; Goldin, *loc. cit.*, p. 152; Moore, *op. cit.*, Vol. I, p. 21; Elbogen, *Der jüdische Gottesdienst in seiner geschichtlichen Entwicklung* (Hildesheim, 1962), p. 36. Kadushin, following Ginzberg and Liebermann, calls attention to earlier forms of the *birkat* directed first against Syria and later against Rome. (Max Kadushin, *Worship and Ethics*, pp. 101–102; Northwestern University Press, 1964; Louis Ginzberg, *A Commentary on the Palestinian Talmud;* Vol. III, pp. 280 f.; New York, 1941; S. Liebermann, *Tosefta Ki-Fshutah, A Comprehensive Commentary on the Tosefta,* Vol. I, p. 54; New York, 1955.)

47. *Babylonian Talmud*, Berakot 29a.

48. *Palestinian Talmud*, Sanhedrin 18.

49. *Midrash Tannaim, Zum Deuteronomium*, ed. by D. Horrmann (Berlin, 1908–1909).

50. Eusebius on Isaiah 18:1.

51. Goldin, *loc. cit.*, p. 135.

52. Justin, *Dialogue* 17, 108; Eusebius on Isaiah 18; Jerome; James Parkes, *The Conflict of the Church and the Synagogue* (London: Soncino Press, 1934), p. 80.

53. Justin, *Dialogue*, 16, 47, 95, 108, 133.

54. *Babylonian Talmud* Ta'anit 27b; Baron, *op. cit.*, Vol. I, p. 134.

55. W. Bacher, *Agada der Tannaiten*, Vol. I, pp. 106–108; Baron, *op. cit.*, p. 148.

56. *Tosefta* Sanhedrin 13, beginning; cf. Bacher, *op. cit.*, pp. 92–93.

57. *Mishnah* Maaser Sheni, 5, 9; Erubin 4, 2; *Tosefta* Sukkah 2, 11; Sifra to Leviticus 23, 40; Sifra to Deut. 43, *Babylonian Talmud* Makkoth 24ab; Exodus Rabba ch. 30. See further by Bacher, *op. cit.*, Vol. I, p. 79; M. Graetz, *History of the Jews* (Philadelphia, 1893), Vol. II, pp. 387–392; Baron, *op. cit.*, Vol. II, p. 135; "Gamaliel II," *Jewish Encyclopedia*, Vol. 5, p. 560.

58. *Midrash Haggadol* Lev. 25, 9; Bacher, *op. cit.*, Vol. II, pp. 82, 83.

59. W. D. Davies, *The Setting of the Sermon on the Mount* (London: Cambridge University Press, 1964), pp. 256–315.

60. *Ibid.*, pp. 310–313.

61. For the best treatment of Matthew's relation to Judaism, see George D. Kilpatrick, *The Origins of the Gospel According to Saint Matthew* (Oxford University Press, 1946), pp. 101–123, and Davies, *op. cit.*, pp. 256–315. For another view, see Günther Bornkamm, Gerhard Barth, and Heinz Joachim Held, *Tradition and Interpretation in Matthew* (The Westminster Press, 1963), and R. Hummel, *Die Auseinandersetzung zwischen Kirche und Judentum in Matthäusevangelium* (Munich, 1963), pp. 32, 33.

62. Kilpatrick, *op. cit.*, pp. 11–113.

63. Joachim Jeremias, *The Parables of Jesus*, tr. by S. H. Hooke (Charles Scribner's Sons, 1963), p. 77.

64. O'Neill, *op. cit.* Cf. Hans Conzelmann, *Die Apostelgeschichte* (Tübingen, 1963); R. P. C. Hanson, *The Acts in the Revised Standard Version* (Oxford University Press, 1967), p. 6; Paul Feine and Johannes Behm, *Introduction to the New Testament*, ed. by Werner G. Kümmel and tr. by A. J. Mattill, Jr. (Abingdon Press, 1966), p. 133.

65. *Ibid.*, pp. 1–53.

66. *Ibid.*, pp. 51–93. Adolf Harnack, *Judentum und Christentum in Justins Dialog mit Trypho* (Leipzig, 1913), T.U. iii 9 (Bank 39), p. 133.

67. Conzelmann's insistence that none of the earlier epochs are models for the time of the church prevents him from seeing adequately Luke's own situation in his description of these

earlier epochs. This is most obvious in the case of the Lord's Supper. Jesus' last supper is clearly the liturgical model for the church's celebration (*op. cit.*, pp. 208–209, 211–213). The sacraments he allows are an exception (*op. cit.*, p. 218).

68. *Mishnah,* Pesahim 10.

69. Hans Lietzmann, *Mass and Lord's Supper,* tr. by D. H. G. Reese (Leiden: Brill, 1926 [German edition]), p. 172.

70. Kirsopp Lake, "The Apostolic Council of Jerusalem," in *The Beginnings of Christianity* (Baker Book House), Vol. 5, p. 207.

71. For a summary of the problem and recent literature, see Hans Conzelmann, *Die Apostelgeschichte,* p. 87.

72. This option is mentioned by Haenchen but rejected for the usual reason that Jewish Christianity had lost all importance since the death of James and the flight to Pella. He does, however, realize that the Council must reflect a time when an attempt was made to settle relations between Jewish and Gentile Christians. (Ernst Haenchen, *Die Apostelgeschichte,* pp. 417–418; Göttingen: Vandenhoeck & Ruprecht, 1956.)

73. O'Neill, *op. cit.,* p. 115. O'Neill concludes: "We should not be surprised that his (Luke) work reflects the situation in the first half of the second century better than it portrays events of the primitive Church." (P. 116.)

74. O'Neill, *op. cit.,* pp. 418–419.

75. *Ibid.,* p. 167, n. 1, 2, 3.

76. Justin, *First Apology,* Ch. 31.

77. Eusebius, *Ecclesiastical History* 4.5.2. According to Arnold Ehrhardt, *The Apostolic Succession in the First Two Centuries of the Church* (London: Lutterworth Press, 1953), pp. 38–39, the list was compiled about 200.

78. Von Campenhausen, *op cit.,* p. 183, n. 4.

79. Eusebius, *Ecclesiastical History* 4. 22. 8.

80. *Ibid.,* 2. 23. 4 ff.

81. *Ibid.,* 3. 22. 2 ff.

82. *Ibid.,* 4. 22. 4.

83. Shlomo Pines, *The Jewish Christians of the Early Centuries of Christianity According to a New Source,* Proceedings of the Israel Academy of Sciences and Humanities, Vol. II, No. 13 (Jerusalem, 1966).

IV

THE ESCHATOLOGICAL PROPHET

Now it is time to turn to an interpretation of Jesus that can take advantage of the concerns expressed in the first three chapters. The first concern was to show how the future world arose. The second concern was to achieve an understanding of the resurrection that would concentrate attention on the importance of the historical Jesus. The third concern was to expose the tragedy of the separation of Christianity and Judaism that forced Christianity to prefer Hellenistic culture over Jewish culture. The advantage of the third concern will be to allow us to find a Jewish Jesus relatively unencumbered by the interpretation placed upon him after the resurrection by New Testament writers who belonged to a church more at home in Hellenistic culture. The second concern has shown that the Jesus we find can be the object of faith before and apart from his resurrection. The third concern enables us to see that Jesus' teaching about the future world was one Jewish way of coping with the world in that day but that we need not repeat it in our day.

The interpretation of Jesus most sympathetic to Jewish culture in Jesus' day was the interpretation of Jesus as "the eschatological prophet." An eschatological prophet was one of the figures expected in late Jewish thought in connection with the end of this world.[1] In him the gift of prophecy was to return so that he might announce the end and prepare Israel for it. The concept of the eschatological prophet is at least as old as the editorial addition to The Book of Malachi which equates the unknown messenger of ch. 3:1 with Elijah. This was a natural development since Elijah was not only the most striking prophet of the Old Testament, but he was also available for another earthly career, having escaped death by translation. With the adoption by Judaism of the idea of a second world, Elijah was provided with a place to reside until the end of the first world. The editor of Malachi was no doubt aware of the passing of prophecy, and Elijah would have seemed the natural candidate to revive it. His second career was to take place immediately "before the great and terrible day of the LORD comes." His task was to "turn the hearts of fathers to their children and the hearts of children to their fathers, lest I come and smite the land with a curse" (Mal. 4:5–6).

Prof. James Muilenburg finds the possibility of the same figure in Isa. 61:1, where he prefers to interpret this anointed figure as a prophet rather than as the servant.[2] "The Spirit of the Lord GOD is upon me, because the LORD has anointed me . . . to proclaim the year of the LORD's favor, and the day of vengeance of our God." (Isa. 61:1–2.) Anointment was the equipment of a prophet in the Old Testament. A messianic role was only indicated where a clear national and political function was required. In both Isa., ch. 61, and Mal., ch. 4, the term "day of the LORD" made a messiah unnecessary. God would come himself to be, as it were, his own messiah.

The outstanding prophet of the Old Testament was Moses. He provided a model as impressive as Elijah for the revival of prophecy at the end. This prophet of the end, modeled on Moses, was supposed to have been promised in Deut., ch. 18, where the author had Moses say, "The LORD your God will raise up for you a prophet like me from among you, from your brethren—him you shall heed" (v. 15). Then the Lord said, "I will raise up for them a prophet like you from among their brethren." (V. 18.) Most probably the author intended to promise an *office* of prophet founded upon the authority and model of Moses.[3] Late Judaism took the passage to mean that a promise of a particular figure like Moses would be the herald of the end.[4] In the process of honoring Moses, late Judaism had furnished him with a translation that avoided death and made him, like Elijah, a candidate for return as the eschatological prophet.

I Maccabees, written sometime during the last two decades of the second century B.C., gives the earliest evidence of a general Jewish belief in the eschatological prophet. Puzzled about the proper disposal of stones from a defiled altar, Jews of the Maccabean period decided to store them "until there should come a prophet to tell what to do with them" (I Macc. 4:46). Thus, the eschatological prophet overshadowed the Maccabean leaders. Simon's office of leader and high priest was termed temporary, "until a trustworthy prophet should arise" (ch. 14:41).

The Qumran literature shows that this group of Essenes also expected the eschatological prophet. In the Manual of Discipline, the rules of the community applied "until the coming of the prophet and the messiahs of Aaron and Israel" (1QS 9:11). The community definitely based part of their expectation on Deut. 18:15–18, where Moses was the model for the eschatological prophet. This passage appeared among the list of Old Testament passages they used to ground their eschatology.[5]

A recently published fragment of Qumran literature has the eschatological prophet replace the other functions of messiah in the Qumran eschatology. In a commentary on Isa. 52:7, the proclaimer is identified as the messiah.[6] This meant that the anointed one at the end had the function of a prophet.

These references concentrate on the idea of the eschatological prophet. The figure becomes clearer when illustrated by men who most probably claimed the office for themselves. One in particular illuminates the idea. Josephus tells of a Jew of Cyrene, named Jonathan, who raised a following among the Jewish poor in the surrounding city.[7] He was of humble origin himself, having been a weaver by trade. No doubt he modeled himself upon Moses, for he persuaded a crowd to follow him into the desert where he would show signs and apparitions. Josephus makes him one of the Sicarii, but he obviously had no revolutionary program in mind because the crowd was unarmed when Roman soldiers fell upon them. Jonathan led them into the desert in expectation of the final eschatological drama which, like the exodus, would occur miraculously there. Unlike messianic figures, the eschatological prophet relied on miracle and the power of God to bring this evil age to its end.

Unless our records of John the Baptist are completely garbled by Christian interests, he is an illustration of the eschatological prophet modeled more upon Elijah than Moses. His clothing, for instance, was the traditional mantle of the prophet which originated with Elijah. And the location of John's ministry in the desert near the Jordan recalls the place where Elijah was translated. His message was an announcement of the end and his baptism, the symbol of preparation for it. Like all other candidates to this office, John found it a dangerous calling. Any eschatological prophet that could muster a following was considered a political threat. According to Josephus, this was the cause of John's death.[8]

This much information about the eschatological prophet shows us that this idea was available among Jews as a possible role or office for Jesus.

It is true that the eschatological prophet was ideologically determined by the future world of late Jewish apocalyptic thought, but this new prophet saw his mission as a mission *in* this world. He was to announce the end for the sake of people who were of this world. He had nothing to do with *executing* the end. His activity did not bring the end but was based on the conviction that the end would come by itself and soon. Particular actions like baptism or leading others out into the desert or to the Jordan were the traditional symbolic actions of the prophet that indicated how totally his life was determined by the truth and impact of his message.[9] The event he proclaimed was so real to him that it was already making its mark upon him. The eschatological prophet himself became a sign in this world of its replacement by the next world.

The eschatological prophet provides a better interpretation of Jesus' earthly career than other possibilities from Jewish culture that were used in the church's Christology. Messiah is simply not descriptive of the nonpolitical, powerless man who died at the hands of a government that a messiah ought to have overthrown.

Oscar Cullmann gives an excellent summary of the Jewish idea of Messiah.[10] He must perform his function on earth. The time of his activity is either the time of the end or a special messianic interim between the old and new worlds. He must be a national, political king, as well as a descendant of David. This title only fits Jesus' history when the power of his resurrection is assumed. Even then, it is a better description of what Jesus has yet to do than what he has accomplished already in history. It only finally fits when we assume that he will come to earth a second time to perform the messianic functions that did not happen during his historic ministry.

It is often claimed that the above idea of Messiah was the common idea in Judaism but that Jesus modified it to include failure, suffering, and death. Jesus is supposed to have gotten this idea of a suffering and dying messiah from certain passages in Isaiah that describe a "suffering servant." First, it must be observed that there was most probably no clear suffering servant figure in the exegesis of the first century. This is mainly the result of the systematic approach of modern Biblical scholars. Secondly, it must be observed that there was no adequate historic occasion to modify the messiah concept to include suffering until this was made necessary by the death of one whose resurrection forced the church to interpret him messianically. For Jesus to have imposed the idea of a suffering messiah upon himself would require a conviction about his own messiahship that has no historical basis. If we were to attribute this idea to Jesus, we should be dealing with the suprahistorical

Christ of the church's confessions rather than the first-century Jew at home in Jewish ideas of the time that serious historical inquiry demands.

These considerations, based on Jewish thinking in Jesus' day, seem confirmed by tradition itself. Jesus resisted every attempt to put him in the role of a messianic freedom fighter who would reinstitute the kingdom of David. The relevant passage is the confession at Caesarea Philippi (Mark 8:27–33). The editorial work of Mark is easily detected. Immediately following Peter's confession, Mark's secrecy theme intrudes in v. 30.[11] In vs. 31 and 32 Mark inserted his own favorite Christology of the Son of Man in a prediction of the passion and resurrection. Mark considered the Son of Man Christology superior to Messiah Christology because it better accounted for the death and resurrection which were not at all provided for in the Jewish idea of Messiah. To point up this inadequacy, Mark had Peter (v. 32) object to the death and resurrection of the Son of Man and receive Jesus' rebuke for preferring Messiah to Son of Man (v. 33).

But if we eliminate Mark's secret, his Son of Man prediction, and Peter's objection (all of which Mark used as a foil for his point of view), we are still left with the rebuke following directly upon Peter's confession. If this analysis is correct, Jesus sharply rejected any possibility of considering him a messiah.[12]

It is probable that the piece as a whole is an editorial construction with the questions of Jesus designed to put forward competing confessions. The rebuke of Peter then becomes simply the continuation of a Marcan polemic against the wing of the church who claimed Peter for their Messiah Christology and against whom Mark championed his own special Son of Man Christology.

The other alleged response of Jesus to Messiahship in the tradition occurs in the passion narrative during the hearing before the Sanhedrin (Mark 14:61–62). In v. 62b, Mark's addition of the Son of Man overpowered the Messiah Christology in a way comparable to the Caesarea Philippi exchange. According to the tradition that came to Mark, Jesus condemned himself by a blasphemous claim to Messiahship. Both Matthew and Luke avoided the outright claim of Jesus, but this is clearly original, because in all three Gospels the result was the same: the high priest concluded from Jesus' answer that he claimed to be Messiah.

On the basis of this confession of Jesus, the Jewish authorities were able to bring Jesus before Pilate on the charge that he was a pretender to the Davidic throne and therefore a threat to Roman sovereignty. Pilate found nothing about Jesus that would indicate he was revolutionary but, even though he recognized that the charge was only an expression of envy, consented to Jewish pressure. This was the explanation of Jesus' crucifixion according to the Synoptic Gospels.

However probable this line of thought might be, it is not historically sound. It is, rather, too neat a combination of condemnation of the Jews and excuse of the Romans. Mark declared his theme of Jewish responsibility for Jesus' death as early as Mark 3:6. As we noted in the previous chapter, this was clearly a part of his plan to appeal to Roman readers by climaxing the passion with the confession of the centurion after absolving Pilate. But the fact remains—almost the only sure one in the whole passion narrative—that Jesus was executed by Rome. We have already given a more probable reason for the accusation than a confession of Jesus to an office that he nowhere else exhibits or claims in his ministry. If he would not make this claim to his own followers or accept the designation when proffered, there is no historical probability that he would have done so with Jewish accusers and the Roman court. Rather than historical, Jesus' confession before the high priest was more apt to have been a dramatic illustration of the dominant motif to which the church subordinated all the pieces of tradition it used to create the passion narrative.[13]

In the light of Jesus' own rejection, current interpretations of Jesus' career have been shifting away from Messiah as a live possibility. The consensus of modern scholars undertaking the new quest of the historical Jesus has been that a messianic self-consciousness for Jesus was not probable. They have suggested instead an indirect Christology. This means a style of life and speech which, by implication, sets Jesus apart from all other men and makes him a unique embodiment of the kind of life the preaching of the church offers. Professor Käsemann finds this specialness in Jesus' overriding of Moses and the Law.[14] Professor Bornkamm finds it in the "unmediated presence" that characterizes Jesus as the one who makes "the reality of God present."[15]

This implicit Christology has resulted in Jesus becoming so special a figure that, like the old Jesus with messianic self-consciousness, he too ceases to be historically probable. There is no cultural setting in which the implicit Christ is at home unless it is as the God-man of the Hellenistic kerygma. The dogmatic captivity of the old quest has returned to haunt the new quest. It will be my contention that data that suggest an "implicit Christology" are better explained by the role of eschatological prophet than by a kerygmatic figure so special that he shatters all possible ways of being a Jew in the first century of our era. This brings us to the Jewishness of the eschatological prophet, but first we must quickly examine the possibility that Jesus thought of himself as the Son of Man.

In Jewish apocalyptic literature, the Son of Man was a preexistent, heavenly figure in the form of a man who would come to earth at the end of time. With the power of heaven he was to turn this world into the perfect world of the apocalyptic, utopian vision. (Dan. 7:13, 15; II Esdras 13; Enoch 46, 48, 52, 69, 71.) Needless to say, there is no possibility of interpreting the Jesus of history in these terms. When Jesus was made to speak of himself as the Son of Man in the Synoptic Gospels, this could only be a reading back of resurrection appearances into the story of Jesus and an expression of the church's expectation of the return of Christ with heavenly powers. There is no Jewish tradition prior to the resurrection that speaks of an earthly career for the apocalyptic Son of Man. Son of Man simply does not match the career of *any* historical figure, let alone the historical Jesus. And now we may take a direct look at the issue of Jesus' Jewishness, which the implicit Christology of the new quest threatens to subvert by casting a Jesus so unique that he belongs to no culture.

The interpretation of Jesus as the eschatological prophet is superior to competing Christologies because it allows the historical Jesus to remain what he most certainly was—a Jew. This lends a historical probability to interpretation which none of the others share to an equal extent. Like Messiah and Son of Man, all the conventional Christological titles require such modification of their original Jewish meaning that they obviously presuppose the resurrection. In this regard, Bultmann's treatment of Jesus is much to be preferred to his disciples. It is better from a historical point of view to have Jesus firmly fixed in Judaism, even though this creates problems for Christian dogma, than to make Jesus smoothly congruent with the kerygma of Paul at the expense of removing him from a believable historical context.

Painful as it may be, the question must be raised whether the new quest does not suffer from a particular cultural bias. It seems to me that it does. This is nowhere clearer than at the basic level of methodological presuppositions. Professor Käsemann accurately expresses the prevailing consensus when he observes that "it is unsafe to predicate authenticity of any passage where there is agreement with contemporary Judaism and/or the post-Easter community."[16] In application this means that, although it is freely granted that Jesus was a Jew, he may not be credited with anything common to Jews. I find the statement of this principle amazing and the general acceptance it has found among the historians who apply it an even greater cause for wonder. Such a methodological presupposition could only result from the dogmatic assumption that Jesus was so unique that he transcends any particular historical nexus. This assumption may do credit to the Christian convictions of the interpreter of Jesus. It, however, does him no credit as a historian.

This methodological approach prejudices the answer to the very question that stimulated the new quest: What is the relation of Jesus to the kerygma of the church? That question can only be answered in an illuminating fashion when the full range of the problem is recognized. Part of that problem is how it came about that Christianity and Judaism became incompatible when the founder of Christianity and all its original adherents were Jews. The methodology of the current investigation of Jesus in effect makes Jesus responsible for the schism even before the issue arose in the history of those times.

Corrected by the fact that Jesus was a Jew, the statement of method should read: It is *safe* to predicate authenticity of any passage in the Gospels that deals with Jesus where there is agreement with contemporary Judaism. When put into effect, this approach throws fresh light on the figure of Jesus by eliminating from serious consideration certain elements in the Jesus tradition that are often used as keystones of interpretation; as when Jesus broke with the Law, or when Jesus put himself above Moses, or when Jesus spoke with unprecedented authority.

Once our method has located Jesus firmly in a Jewish milieu, there is hope that a form of Christianity may emerge from this foundation that will not feel compelled to break with Judaism. The fact that Jesus was a Jew and not the first Christian could recall contemporary Christians to the original situation of the church when it was possible to be both Jew and Christian at the same time. It is intolerably sad that the division and hostility between Jew and Christian should continue merely because separation seemed wise in the '80s and '90s of our era. The weary tragedy of centuries of conflict cannot of course be relieved by the effort of any one generation of reconciliation. But Jesus the Jew might at least remove the barrier in principle.

One further advantage might be gained from a Jesus at home in Judaism. It seems to me that Jewish culture has greater affinities to modern secular culture than the Hellenistic culture, which became the vehicle of orthodoxy. Like modern, secular, empirical, Anglo-Saxon culture, Jewish culture was more functional than ontological. Like modern scientific culture, Judaism was more interested in what something was for than what it was in itself. Consequently, a form of Christianity built upon a Jewish Jesus should make it easier to devise modern equivalents to first-century Christianity than a Christianity built upon the metaphysical, ontological models of Hellenistic culture.

These obvious advantages of the eschatological prophet approach to Jesus are enough to encourage an attempt at an application to the tradition about Jesus. But one decisive reservation remains. Almost all current interpreters reject the eschatological prophet approach because it does not adequately provide for the uniqueness of Jesus.[17] This, I think, is the common denominator to all the objections to the adequacy of this title for Jesus. It is crucial to note, though, that these objections arise, not because the concept itself is inadequate, but rather, because of a failure to appreciate how unique the eschatological prophet was in the conceptual framework where the idea was at home.

In the vast majority of cases where the idea occurs in Jewish eschatology, the eschatological prophet has a completely unique function. He is God's last word before the end of history. No one will come after him but God himself. No other historical figure is provided for. The eschatological prophet is as *sui generis* in the framework of Jewish eschatology as the God-man of the councils of the church is in the framework of a revised Platonic metaphysics. One thing that makes this difficult to appreciate for Christians is the traditional assignment of the eschatological prophet role to John the Baptist. This makes the eschatological prophet merely the forerunner of the really decisive figure. But in the eschatological scheme which I am discussing, there is no messiah who comes afterward. The eschatological prophet is the sole historical agent connected with the end. To draw the analogy with the God-man Christology, the eschatological prophet relates to the line of the prophets like the God-man relates to mankind. And the eschatological prophet relates uniquely to the final act of God like the God-man relates uniquely to the nature of God. As this second relation is sometimes put, the eschatological prophet is uniquely functional while the God-man is uniquely ontological. In their respective frameworks of thought, they are equally unique and exalted.

There is no intention here of advocating a lower status for Jesus than the conventional Christology. To many people this is what prophet connotes. It seems to be a way by which Jesus is reduced to being just one of the prophets. But this overlooks the specialness of the *eschatological* prophet. He is no more merely another prophet than the Christ of conventional doctrine is merely another man simply because he shares the nature of men. The eschatological prophet is the full analogous equivalent of the God-man. The differences are attributable to the difference between Jewish culture's frame of reference and a Hellenistic cultural setting. If this fully unique status is granted to the eschatological prophet concept as a whole, then some particular objections can be dealt with.

Professor Bornkamm seems to require that the prophet category completely contain Jesus. This is an unreasonable requirement. No historical category completely contains any historical figure. All that may reasonably be expected from a specific historical category is that it best illumine the figure in question. Each person has a variety of roles and his particularity is never completely explained by any of them. But eschatological prophet certainly illumines the authority and unmistakable otherness of Jesus which Bornkamm finds to be the special characteristics of Jesus.

Professor Käsemann's objection is more substantial. He feels that Jesus broke with the Law and set himself above Moses in a way a prophet could never do. I shall show that Jesus did not break with the Law, that he did not make Moses obsolete or reduce his importance, and that whatever criticisms Jesus did make of Law are the natural expressions of his function as the eschatological prophet.

Professor Cullmann's objection raises the question of orthodoxy in a way that is especially important for our discussion. When he objects to the eschatological prophet not adequately providing for the activity of the risen Christ, he implies that this was the decisive phase of the activity of Christ for the whole primitive church. This is most probably not true. The activity of the risen Christ was decisive only for the Hellenistic church which modeled its religious experience upon the Hellenistic redeemer who dies but rises to be with the believer. The Jewish wing of the church by contrast used eschatological models; that is, the eschatological prophet and Son of Man. For these, the decisive activity was either the past career of Jesus as the eschatological prophet or the future action of the Son of Man at the end of the age, not the redeemer contemporary with the believer. It so happens that the literature of the New Testament overwhelmingly reflects the Hellenistic style of Christianity and, because it was the style most congenial to the culture of the Roman Empire, it came to dominate the history of the church. This does not mean that the Hellenistic wing of the church was orthodox and the Jewish wing heretical. That would be ridiculous in the light of the primacy of the Jewish wing of the church. As Luke informs us, it was the Jerusalem church that gave its approval to Paul and the Gentile mission. It is one of the great ironies of history that the Western, Hellenistic wing of the church eventually suppressed the Jewish wing that gave it birth and permitted it to develop.

We have reviewed the tragic story that produced this sad turn of events. It would appear to be absurdly irrelevant to perpetuate the subapostolic prejudice against Jewish Christianity, once the historic factors are known. Professor Cullmann is in danger of repeating this prejudice when he remarks that the only Christological system we know, built entirely upon the

foundation of the eschatological prophet, belonged to a heretical branch of early Christianity—the one found in the Pseudo-
Clementine *Preaching of Peter*.[18] Fortunately, in the same discussion of Jesus the prophet, Professor Cullmann readily admits
that this is one of the oldest Christologies. He would surely
not wish to condemn all of Jewish Christianity to heresy because one branch of it became Gnostic. It is a historical accident that the source where the most developed statement of
prophet Christology is preserved is the Pseudo-Clementine literature. Surely the prophet Christology was preserved also by
Jewish Christians who were not Gnostics. The fact is that there
are very few records of any kind left by the continuing Jewish Christian church.

The implications of Professor Käsemann's oblique comments
about early Jewish Christianity seem to shut out the possibility
of a legitimate Christology in that mold. He warns against the
danger of falling back into an Ebionite type of Jewish Christianity as a result of many current conversations with Israel
and of what he sees as a Judaizing tendency in theology. This
is understandable in the light of his theory that it was the Hellenistic church that really appreciated Jesus' break with the
Law; which break, Jesus' closest followers seem to have
missed.[19] And, the historic probability is that Jesus' companions
understood him best.

No one would wish to deny that a vigorous Jewish Christian
church continued as the legitimate heir of the Jerusalem church
of James and Peter long after the Western church centered in
Rome reckoned it among the heretics. Strecker has shown that
the variety within this church in Syria was too great for it to
be covered by any single sect description such as "Ebionite,"
and that it may very well have been the dominant orthodox
position in that geographical area.[20]

Our knowledge of the history of Jewish Christianity has been
greatly enriched by the records of Jewish Christianity embedded in a text by the Islamic author, 'Abd al-Jabbār, recently
discovered in Istanbul by Prof. Shlomo Pines, of the Hebrew

University in Jerusalem.[21] He estimates that these texts represent Jewish Christians of the fifth or the sixth century. According to this text, the Jewish Christians resented the victory of the Roman church and felt that it had been achieved at the expense of assimilating the religion of Jesus to the culture of Rome. According to their tradition, they were a continuation of the original Jerusalem church. They regretted the split between Judaism and Christianity. According to their doctrine, Jesus had kept the commandments of Moses and was a man, not a divine being. The Christology seemed to be that of the eschatological prophet. Portions of the texts quoted by Professor Pines make clear that the authors believed there was something special about Christ compared to other Jews. "There was a disagreement between them and the Jews with regard to Christ."[22] Two passages indicate that this disagreement was over the question whether or not Jesus was *the* prophet. The first passage states that the Jewish Christian group of the Istanbul texts modeled their gospel upon the pattern of the Old Testament stories of the "births of the prophets and of the histories of their lives."[23] The other passage coupled Jesus with the prophets by pointing out the common use of Hebrew by "Christ and the prophets before him."[24]

The 'Abd al-Jabbār text shows that these Jewish Christians considered themselves truer followers of Jesus than the orthodox church of the West. Given their cultural affinity with the Jewishness of Jesus, the historical probability is on their side.

When we turn to the New Testament itself, there is convincing evidence that the later Jewish Christians who believed in Jesus as the eschatological prophet were building on a view of Jesus current in the church of New Testament times. In our treatment of the story of Peter's confession at Caesarea Philippi, we have already noted that the story as it stands in Mark, ch. 8, is probably an editorial composition rather than a unit of early tradition. The structuring of the incident upon the artificial questions of Jesus, "Who do men say that I am?" and "But who do you say that I am?" makes it most probably Mark's way of setting up the comparison of competing Christologies, and that this was the real theme of the exchange between Jesus and the disciples. It is quite out of the character expressed in the rest of tradition for Jesus to be concerned for his own person, let alone to draw others' attention to the subject. The composition speaks of three Christologies and of three groups who champion them. They are the Christology of the eschatological prophet (John the Baptist, Elijah, or one of the prophets) believed by "men," the Christology of Messiah championed by Peter, and the Christology of the Son of Man advanced by Mark.

"Men" must have represented a community in the church with the Christology of the eschatological prophet. The models for this Christology occur in Mark 6:14 f., where Herod and "others" think Jesus may be John the Baptist raised from the dead, or "Elijah," or "a prophet, like one of the prophets of old." The second occurrence of eschatological prophet in Mark referring to "some," "Herod," and "others," together with the first reference to "men," shows that Mark is mounting a polemic against this doctrine. Whom was he combating? It is clear that the group in question were believers in Jesus. They did not dismiss him as a fraud or as one who worked wonders by the power of Satan. They were not the hostile Jews in the story of the Beelzebul accusation (ch. 3:22 ff.). The Jews in Mark did not credit Jesus with being a prophet. This was confirmed in the passion narrative incident at the ninth hour when the spectators thought Jesus might have been calling for Elijah (ch. 15:3 ff.). They would not suppose this if they believed that Jesus was Elijah in person. The Elijah legends of later Judaism gave that prophet the role of heavenly helper and intercessor for those in need.[25] Those who believed Jesus was the eschatological prophet were not hostile or indifferent Jews. They were believers in Jesus.

When Jesus returned to his own country, Mark again showed

us a prophet Christology (Mark 6:1 ff.). After being ridiculed as a carpenter with prophetic pretensions, Jesus pronounced the word about the prophet without honor in his own country. Mark connected this with believing acceptance of Jesus as a miracle worker. "And he could do no mighty work there." (V. 5.) Here Mark was willing to include a saying about Jesus as prophet because it served his purpose of illustrating Jesus' rejection at home.

Who, then, were these believing Jews whose Christology ranked below Peter? They must have been the Jewish Christians whom Mark was bound to reject because they were observant of the Law while Mark wished to use Jesus as the basis of his rejection of it (Mark 2:28; 7:1 ff.). His other reason for rejecting this title for Jesus was because he used it to dispose of John the Baptist as a possible competitor to Jesus (ch. 9:13). By making John the forerunner of the Messiah instead of the last one before the end, Mark, following an eschatological pattern similar to that of the Qumran community, both adequately honored John and effectively disposed of the eschatological prophet Christology.

Mark was engaged in a polemic against the prophet Christology in more subtle ways. It is probable that some of his most important pericopes originally served to convey just this Christology but have been modified to support another point of view. The Baptism and the transfiguration deserve special attention in this connection.[26]

The Baptism in its present form is a legend of the consecration of the Messiah[27] (Mark 1:9–11). As Bultmann suggests, it is most probably the work of the Hellenistic church where baptism went together with the giving of the Spirit. Accordingly, the story of Jesus' receipt of the Spirit was connected to the baptism of Jesus by Mark. The editorial connection of the two events was accomplished in ch. 1:8, where Mark has John say, "I have baptized you with water; but he will baptize you with the Holy Spirit." Matthew and Luke had simply, "He will baptize you with the Holy Spirit and with fire" (Matt. 3:11b; Luke

3:16b). To baptize with the Spirit, Jesus had first to receive the Spirit, so Mark made the connection.

The baptismal legend comes to a climax in the Voice from heaven which identified Jesus as the Messiah by using the enthronement Psalm 2, "You are my son, today I have begotten you" (Ps. 2:7). This is coupled with Isa. 42:1a, "Behold my servant, whom I uphold, my chosen, in whom my soul delights," which is connected to bestowal of the Spirit in v. 1b, "I have put my Spirit upon him." This Voice from heaven is the creation of Mark because a similar voice said almost the same thing at the transfiguration (Mark 9:7). The Voice is Mark's way of specifying his own meaning and fending off other possible interpretations of the bestowal of the Spirit upon Jesus.

Another possible interpretation immediately suggests itself when the story is stripped of Mark's editorial work; that is, when we remove the connection with John's baptism and the interpreting voice. The result is: "Immediately he saw the heavens opened and the Spirit descending upon him like a dove." Now the legend reveals an apocalyptic vision at its core. The "opened heavens" recall Stephen's vision in Acts 7:56: "Behold, I see the heavens opened." This is typical of apocalyptic visions and has had special eschatological significance ever since its use in Isa. 64:1: "O that thou wouldst rend the heavens and come down." Mark's word for "opening" or "tearing" connotes a sudden tearing open of heaven like the tearing of the curtain of the Temple at the crucifixion which gives emphasis to the eschatological significance. The splitting of heaven was to let the Spirit descend at the end of the age. Until the end the Spirit was confined to heaven, having been withdrawn with the disappearance of the prophets.

Mark took the primitive report of an apocalyptic vision and put it into narrative form. If we reconvert it into direct discourse, it becomes a perfect parallel in form to the single example in the Synoptic tradition of an authentic report of a vision of Jesus:[28]

I saw the heavens torn and the Spirit descending like a dove. (Mark 1:10.)
I saw Satan fall like lightning from heaven. (Luke 10:18.)

The reconstruction of the original vision report assumes that the *euthus* in this case is part of Mark's connection of the vision to the baptism. Also the *eis auton* is most probably added since Jesus' report of the vision as his own would be enough indication that the event relates specifically to him.

Mark showed shrewd judgment in placing this vision at the beginning of Jesus' ministry, although it does not fit the usual pattern for the call of a prophet. Apparently no call story was available. But this vision does explain the source and significance of Jesus' activity. The fulfillment of the eschatological promise of the return of the Spirit signals the eschatological significance of the one who sees it return. It implies that the ministry of the one who sees it has its source in this Spirit, just as the vision of Satan's fall from heaven implied that the one who saw that event was directly involved in it. In fact, the two visions are strikingly complementary. Satan was thrown down from heaven because the Spirit had descended from heaven. The comparison with lightning shows the one event as a judgment. The comparison with a dove reveals the other as a gift of grace.[29]

The conclusion is that Jesus had a vision of the return of the Spirit to earth that both designated and qualified him for the task of the eschatological prophet. In Judaism, the gift of the Spirit was primarily a bestowal of the gift of prophecy. It was associated with the role of messiah only when that role was particularly specified. That role was not involved in Jesus' original vision. Mark added the messiah role from his post-resurrection perspective.

When we turn to the story of the transfiguration, we can recognize Mark's theological interest from our analysis of the confession of Peter which went immediately before. Again Mark used the incident to confirm his Son of Man Christology.

The conversation coming down from the mountain forbade the disciples to relate what they had seen until the Son of Man had risen (Mark 9:9). From his own commentary we can see that Mark considered this a resurrection story, which justifies Bultmann's description of it as a resurrection legend. But if we ask, what the disciples specifically saw that made it a *resurrection* legend, Mark's editorial addition is exposed. Only the metamorphosis of v. 3 makes Jesus into a heavenly being; that is, a resurrected being after the pattern of the Son of Man. Mark added this to the story that came to him to make it confirm his Son of Man Christology. Two things expose this metamorphosis as an addition. Peter showed no reaction to the transformed Jesus. He addressed him simply as "Rabbi," as a historical figure. Mark's description of the garments as so white "no fuller *on earth* could bleach them" (italics added) shows that now Jesus was not on earth. Mark had shown in his first mention of the Son of Man that "on earth" is not the natural location of this figure. When he had Jesus forgive sin as the Son of Man, he explained that "the Son of man has authority *on earth* to forgive sins" (ch. 2:10; italics added). The phrase was the same in both places.[30]

Another interest of Mark carries over from the story of the confession of Peter. That story began with the rejection of an Elijah or eschatological prophet Christology. The interpretative conversation coming down the mountain made the same point in the designation of John the Baptist as Elijah (Mark 9:11–13). This shows that Mark was afraid that the appearance of the two figures who were the models for the eschatological prophet in late Jewish eschatology might suggest that they were passing this role on to Jesus. This polemic of Mark alerts us to the prophet Christology thrust of the story before Mark edited it for his purposes. This indeed is what Peter communicated with the three eschatological booths.[31] Peter's action made Jesus the prophet like Moses and like Elijah. Mark undid this by the addition of v. 6, "He did not know what to say, for they were exceedingly afraid." He carried over the theme of the mistaken Peter from the confession scene. He carried back their unsettling fear from the empty tomb story in which the women were so frightened that they failed to report their experience (Mark 16:8).[32]

In the original story, the Voice from heaven confirmed Peter's interpretation of Jesus as eschatological prophet. But Mark's insertion of Peter's confusion made the Voice correct Peter instead. To justify Peter being corrected, Mark added the transfiguration. The result was that, whereas the Voice from the cloud originally confirmed the interpretation of Jesus as eschatological prophet, now it declared this to be a mistake and Jesus to be another figure altogether.

But Mark left at least one element in the Voice as it came to him that betrayed its original import: "Listen to him." This is a quotation of Deut. 18:15b, the source for the doctrine of the Mosaic eschatological prophet. Mark probably changed the first part of the message of the Voice to conform to the message of the Voice at the baptism, although Ferdinand Hahn thinks he detects an original allusion to Isa. 42:1 that supports the prophet motif.[33]

A historical analysis of these two very important pieces of Synoptic tradition has exposed a substratum of tradition that served an eschatological prophet Christology. The other Gospels confirm the existence of a community with this Christology. With the evidence of Mark before us, we must assume that traces of this doctrine in other Gospels are not idiosyncrasies or creations of any particular Gospel but further proof that the very early Jewish Christian church championed this point of view.

It is interesting to find a passage in Q that confirms a uniqueness of the eschatological prophet similar to the uniqueness of the God-man. Q applies the uniqueness to John, but the point holds good for Jesus when the eschatological prophet is applied to him. "Why then did you go out? To see a prophet? Yes, I tell you, and more than a prophet." (Matt. 11:9; Luke 7:26.) The text goes on to specify this specialness in the fulfillment of the role of the eschatological prophet described in Mal. 3:1. As the eschatological prophet, Jesus was more than a prophet.

Luke was the Synoptic author most open in his preservation of a prophet Christology, partly because of his reconciling attitude to the early Jewish Christian church that sponsored this doctrine and partly because it made Jesus nonpolitical. Consequently, Luke gave us one of the few pieces of truly biographical material available in the tradition. It is the biographical apothegm at Luke 13:31–33 about Jesus and Herod.[34] The point of the incident for our purposes is that Jesus considered death a natural part of his office as a prophet. Luke employed this for a nonpolitical explanation of Jesus' death.[35] Here, most probably, is the earliest explanation of the crucifixion, before postresurrection theories of fulfillment of prophecy and some kind of atonement developed. This apothegm, coupled with the vision at the heart of the baptism legend, put the whole ministry of Jesus in a historically probable framework.

Luke's interest in the eschatological prophet led him to explain the whole ministry of Jesus in these terms by shifting the rejection at Nazareth to the beginning of the Galilean ministry. Luke then added Isa. 61:1–2 from his fund of testimonia. The Isaiah quotation described the role of the eschatological prophet. In this fashion, he built upon the original reference in the tradition to the prophet unacceptable in his own country (Luke 4:16 ff.).

Luke also advanced a prophet Christology in the story of the woman with the ointment (Luke 7:39) and in the resurrection story of the two disciples on the way to Emmaus who looked back on Jesus of Nazareth as "a prophet mighty in deed and word before God and all the people" (ch. 24:19).

Consideration of Luke's position in his Gospel raises the question of the same subject in his second volume. In Acts there is a description of Jesus as the Mosaic eschatological prophet which does not reflect primarily Luke's apologetic for a nonpolitical messiah who would not threaten the Roman state. Peter's speech in Solomon's porch quoted Deut. 18:15 f.

to explain Jesus' career, as did Stephen (Acts 3:22; 7:37). In these instances, there is a high probability that Luke was using sources that reflected the tradition of the earliest Jewish Christian church.[36] The motif of the nonpolitical Messiah is much less likely to be important in Acts than in the Gospel. In Acts, the relation of the church to Rome is more important than the relation of Jesus to Rome.

If we put the evidence of an eschatological prophet approach to Jesus in the Synoptic Gospels and Acts together with the position of the author of the Fourth Gospel, the stage is set for a modest exploration of this approach to Jesus. The Gospel of John denied the role of the eschatological prophet to John the Baptist because of a conflict between followers of the Baptist and John's church. Instead the title was given to Jesus (John 1:21, 25; 6:14.)[37] This does not mean, of course, that prophet was the major Christology for John and his church. It does mean that the title "eschatological prophet" was important and unique enough to compete with other Christologies of the church. This is the best evidence we have of the power of this Christology to match the Christologies that became the vehicles of orthodoxy. Now let us see how this approach to Jesus affects our understanding of him.

To understand a prophet is to understand his message. Jesus' message was simply and adequately summarized by Mark: "The kingdom of God is at hand" (Mark 1:15). The Kingdom of God was Jesus' vision of salvation. The nearness of this Kingdom was the driving power behind his mission. His ethical demands and his style of life were implications drawn directly from the nearness of this Kingdom.

The tradition about Jesus gives no special definition of the Kingdom. Jesus seemed to have assumed that his hearers knew what he meant. For Jesus, the Kingdom of God stood for the future world in which God would reign, and in which he would bring to realization the promised salvation.[38] This was the primary sense of the term as Jesus used it and explains why Jesus spoke of "entering the kingdom of God" (Mark 9:47;

10:23 ff.), or of "sons of the kingdom" (Matt. 8:12), or of "inheriting the kingdom" (ch. 25:34) when Judaism would ordinarily have used "world to come" instead of "kingdom of God" in these connections.

The primacy of the future aspect of the Kingdom of God in Jesus' message is generally recognized among scholars.[39] But this admission seems to produce anxiety lest the Kingdom be so future that it rob the career of Jesus of adequate redemptive significance. This anxiety manifests itself in an overwhelming interest in the question of how much the Kingdom is future and how much it is present.[40] It is, of course, legitimate to deal with this important issue. But a distorted idea of the Kingdom results if this is taken to be the most important thing about the Kingdom. The most important thing about the Kingdom in the teaching of Jesus is its scope. Once the scope is clear, other questions find appropriate answers.

When Jesus used the Kingdom of God to mean the future world where God would reign, the scope is clearly implied. The Kingdom of God was to be the total solution to the problems of the world and of all mankind. God would provide this solution in a single, omnipotent act. In the nature of the case, the bringing of the Kingdom had to be the act of God because no human agency was adequate to such a task. This is why, in Jesus' teaching, man had nothing whatever to do with bringing the Kingdom or even hastening its arrival. Man's only role in relation to the Kingdom's coming was to repent in preparation for it (Mark 1:15) and to long for it in prayer (Matt. 6:12; Luke 11:2).

Just two facets of the Kingdom that Jesus proclaimed make clear how global, even cosmic, the scope of it was for him. In his one most probably authentic vision, Jesus saw "Satan fall like lightning from heaven" (Luke 10:18). This implied that the new world of the Kingdom would be free of the influence of God-contrary powers. There would be no demon possession since the demons were the agents of Satan (Mark 3:22 ff.). There would be no supranatural agency in the world to oppose

God or to lead men to misinterpret his will as in the stories of the temptation of Jesus (ch. 1:13) and of Peter's misunderstanding at Caesarea Philippi (ch. 8:33). The Kingdom of God implied the elimination of the major source of evil in the universe.[41]

Another facet of the Kingdom that illumined its scope was Jesus' expectation for the Gentiles' part in it. As Jeremias has so excellently shown, Jesus limited his own activity to the "lost sheep of the house of Israel" (Matt. 15:24) and forbade his disciples to minister to Gentiles (ch. 10:5 f.).[42] On the other hand, his vision included the conversion of the Gentiles by the same act of God that would bring the Kingdom, so that finally "many will come from east and west and sit at table with Abraham, Isaac, and Jacob" (Matt. 8:11; Luke 13:28). Jesus promised the Gentiles a share in the salvation of the Kingdom when it would come at the end of the age. There was to be a miraculous gathering in of the nations as in the visions of the latter Old Testament prophets. Given that the Kingdom involved this kind of event in Jesus' teaching, it must have been primarily future, since these events certainly did not happen in his ministry. It follows that any discussion of the sense in which the Kingdom was present in Jesus' ministry must be a derivative of the basic concept and not its equivalent. Also any sense in which the Kingdom was present in Jesus' activity must not be allowed to reduce the Kingdom to triviality compared to the scope it had in its basically future form.

There are indications that Jesus had to counter attempts to belittle the full scope of the Kingdom in his message. The point of the parable of the mustard seed is the contrast between the size of the mustard seed and the size of the full-grown mustard tree. In Mark's setting, the mustard seed would be the same as the seed in his explanation of the parable of the sower at the beginning of the chapter—the seed of the word which the church spreads in its mission. Then the full-grown shrub would represent "the mighty host of the people of God in the Messianic Age."[43]

In the probable original setting of this parable, the subject was the Kingdom apart from any association with the mission of the church. The eschatological prophet did not anticipate time for a mission. Then it would have been a parable of assurance, but not assurance of the ultimate success of the mission. Instead, it provided assurance that the Kingdom to come would be as grand as Jesus proclaimed it would be, in spite of the modesty of his ministry.

The companion parable of the leaven makes the same point and requires the same original setting (Matt. 13:33; Luke 13:20).

Jesus' rejection of Peter's attempt to designate him Messiah at Caesarea Philippi in the original apothegm version of that story also expressed an awareness of the incongruity of the modesty of Jesus' activity as compared to the Kingdom he proclaimed. The attempt to make Jesus Messiah was an attempt to turn the Kingdom of God into a program of political activity. This was too small an enterprise compared to the Kingdom in Jesus' message.

The disproportion between Jesus' activity as a prophet and the cataclysmic context of his message must have been behind the demands for a sign. His hearers wanted to see something that was a preview of the magnitude of the coming Kingdom. But Jesus refused to give any signs except those which would authenticate him as a prophet like Jonah (Matt. 12:39; Luke 11:29).[44] The request is significant in itself, for it shows that Jesus' hearers understood what kind of scope the "kingdom" included for Jesus and wished some confirmation of that scope immediately.

The cosmic, eschatological scope of the Kingdom of God in the teaching of Jesus corresponds to the compass of that concept in late Jewish eschatology.[45] In Jewish thought, the Kingdom of God was the goal of history to be revealed at the end to all flesh (Isa. 40:5). Then God would become the *de facto,* active, visible ruler of the whole world. Every living thing would praise and worship him exclusively. The kingdom of this world which opposed the Kingdom of God would disappear. The one true religion confessing the one true God would become the religion of all the nations. This scope explains why the Kingdom, of necessity, had to be primarily future for Jesus. Until the total situation of mankind in the universe would change to the extent that the Kingdom of God prescribed, it had to remain future. But this is not the most important point of the scope of the Kingdom.

The most important point of the scope of the Kingdom for an understanding of Jesus' career is that this scope is what made Jesus' message interesting. What he promised would affect everything and everyone. No one could exempt himself from its influence. It was the unavoidable destiny of the universe.

In the postresurrection theologies of the Gospels, Jesus himself was made the focus of interest as the Messiah, or the Son of Man, or the eternal Logos. In these roles, his person was most important because he dispensed eschatological salvation, in a preliminary way in his earthly career and finally at his return. But as a fully historical figure in the role of eschatological prophet, Jesus attracted attention to himself only insofar as he displayed the credentials of a prophet. His message was the important thing to which he called attention. Jesus' followers attached themselves to his conception of the Kingdom of God. They did not follow him out of personal attachment. This would have been to miss the point of his mission as the eschatological prophet. Of course, to believe his message it was necessary to relate to him as the eschatological prophet. But this was not the primary relationship. The primary relationship involved in Jesus' proclamation of the Kingdom was the relationship to the King of that Kingdom, whom Jesus called Father. It is important to clarify Jesus' relation to the message of the Kingdom of God because the scope of the Kingdom is often lost when an intimate, individual relationship with Jesus is substituted for a relationship with the Kingdom and its King.

After scope, the next most important feature of the Kingdom

was its nearness. This explains the urgency and radical character of Jesus' ethical demands. There was a certain logic to the nearness of the Kingdom. If God was powerful and cared about his people, he would have to act soon for their redemption. But we do not know what considerations actually led Jesus to his conviction that the end was near. John the Baptist may have been an important influence in this regard. What we do know is that in all probability Jesus was the founder of the church's sense of the nearness of the end. Jesus taught the nearness of the Kingdom in many ways.

We have already noted the nearness of the Kingdom in the summary of Jesus' preaching: "The kingdom of God has come near" (Mark 1:15; Matt. 4:17). The same Greek verb for "has come near" occurs in a Q saying (Matt. 10:7; Luke 10:9) in connection with the missionary charge to the disciples. Matthew followed Mark. Luke added, "the kingdom of God has come near to *you*." In all these cases, the perfect of the verb "to come near" has the established meaning of "has come near" or "is at hand."[46] The use of this verb in the summaries of Mark and Matthew both for Jesus and for John the Baptist shows that these Evangelists understood that this was the primary time consideration in Jesus' conception of the Kingdom.

The nearness of the Kingdom in Jesus' teaching was confirmed by parables to this effect like the one about the fig tree (Mark 13:28 f.; Matt. 24:32 f.; Luke 21:29–31). That particular parable called attention to the new leaves of a fig tree that heralded the nearness of summer. Mark and Matthew applied it to the nearness of the coming of the Son of Man on clouds in the preceding paragraph; Luke applied it instead to the nearness of the Kingdom of God, although his preceding paragraph also dealt with the return of the Son of Man. But little can be concluded from the setting of the parable in the eschatological discourses of the Gospels because they were editorial compositions. If we remove the applications given to the parable in the discourses, nothing telling can be brought against its authenticity.[47] The parable remains an eschatological one when lifted out of its Gospel setting because it belongs to the harvest theme which was frequently used to symbolize the *eschaton*.[48] Its point was that the end is as near as summer is to the time of the sprouting fig tree.

The other parable stressing the nearness of the Kingdom with good claim to authenticity is the thief in the night (Matt. 24:43-44; Luke 12:39-40).[49] The concluding reference to the coming of the Son of Man is the product of the church, for, as Vielhauer has shown, the coming Son of Man has no place in Jesus' message of the Kingdom.[50] The injection of the coming Son of Man into Jesus' teaching is the church's way of making Jesus the object of faith, where in his own message the coming Kingdom of God had been the object of hope. The sayings about the coming of the Son of Man in the church's theology have, then, indirect value as a witness to the nearness of the Kingdom in Jesus' message. Since Bultmann takes the future sayings about the Son of Man to be authentic, he does not detect the work of the church in this parable. But Jeremias is alerted to this by the absence of the application to the Son of Man in the parallel from the Gospel of Thomas.[51]

Without the Son of Man interpretation, the parable of the thief in the night states simply that the thief—the intrusion of the Kingdom into this world—will come in a watch of the night or at an hour that is unexpected. "You also must be ready." Jeremias finds parallels to this call to readiness for the nearness of the Kingdom in the parables of the flood (Matt. 24:34 ff.; Luke 17:26 f.) and the destruction of Sodom (Luke 17:28 ff.).

Perhaps the clearest indirect evidence for the nearness of the Kingdom in Jesus' teaching is the request for signs this raised. Since Jesus proclaimed the imminence of the final eschatological drama, it was natural to expect that he would give some proof for his claim by pointing out its opening scenes. Jesus distinguished himself from other apocalyptists by simply refusing such proof while still insisting the truth of his claim that the end was near (Mark 8:12; Matt. 12:39 f.; Luke 11:29 f.).

There is no need to extend the discussion to include all the possible evidence for the imminent future of the Kingdom of God in Jesus' teaching. This has been admirably done by Kümmel and is readily available in his *Promise and Fulfillment.* What we wish to do is to move to our next step, which is to illuminate the way Jesus' ethical teaching was determined by this Kingdom, cosmic in scope, and near in time.

The eschatological prophet called for repentance in the light of his message about the Kingdom. As we have noted, the main concern of a prophet is his message. We would expect, then, that the ethics of Jesus were implied in that message. The relationship between the two can be stated simply. For Jesus, ethics was the way of life that would prevail when the Kingdom would come. Ethics was the shape of life in the future Kingdom. This way of life was obligatory even before the Kingdom would come. To live according to the requirements of the Kingdom was to live in such a fashion already that one would be at home in the Kingdom when it came suddenly and unexpectedly.

This means that the disciple of the future Kingdom would be out of place until the Kingdom came. To be prepared to be at home in the circumstance of the future world is to be condemned to being a displaced person in this world, because its way of life and its circumstances are not the circumstances and way of life in the Kingdom. This dislocation must be borne and can be borne because the time of the world is short and because the only ones who may live in the future Kingdom will be the ones who are ready for it. To be ready for it means to be practicing its way of life already. Put another way, the ethics of the Kingdom required that a man live as if the Kingdom of God were already come and as if the world were not the way it still is.

We noticed above that Jesus did not define his doctrine of the Kingdom of God but seemed to assume that his hearers knew what he meant. Now we are in a position to improve that description of Jesus' doctrine. Jesus did not describe the Kingdom of God pictorially as might have been expected, but he did give a clear definition of it. His concrete description of the Kingdom was in his ethics. This was his reading of what life in the Kingdom would be like. Jesus' teaching on sexuality and politics best illustrate the relation between Kingdom and ethics.

If we begin by asking which saying of Jesus comes closest to describing the role of sexuality in the future Kingdom of God, the conversation with the Sadducees about the resurrection provides the answer (Mark 12:18 f.; Matt. 22:23 f.; Luke 20:27 f.). At this point, Bultmann becomes an unreliable guide to authenticity because of his prejudice against Jesus' sharing anything in common with the rabbis.[52] The eschatological prophet was faithful to Law but interpreted it eschatologically. As Lohmeyer recognizes, precisely because there is a Jewish doctrine of life after death in this pericope and not the early church's belief in resurrection, it is probably an authentic reflection of Jesus' teaching.[53] Luke in particular assumes the resurrection of the just only. As Bultmann admits, there is little likelihood that Sadducees would have challenged the early church the way this unit of tradition does.

For our purposes the important text is: "For when they rise from the dead, they neither marry nor are given in marriage, but are like angels in heaven." (Mark 12:25; Matt. 22:30; Luke 20:34–35; Enoch 51:4; 104:6; Apoc. of Baruch 51:10.) According to Jesus, there was no sexuality in the Kingdom of God and those committed to the Kingdom should prepare accordingly. All of Jesus' teaching on sexuality followed from this fundamental aspect of his vision of the future Kingdom.

Matthew 19:12 approves of those who "made themselves eunuchs for the sake of the kingdom of heaven." Approval of this style of life results from the fact that a eunuch eliminates his sexuality and thus conforms to the life of the Kingdom already even before it comes.[54] Naturally, he will be received into the future Kingdom.

The same vision of the Kingdom accounted for Jesus' opinion on divorce and remarriage. It is not easy to decide which version of Jesus' teaching on this subject was original. The passages in question actually dealt with two issues instead of one. Mark 10:11 most probably preserved the original tradition, but v. 12 was modified to relate to the practice of a wife divorcing her husband—an option only available in Greco-Roman culture but inconceivable in the Jewish Palestinian context of Jesus.[55] The issue here was remarriage, not divorce. Divorce was permitted on condition that remarriage did not follow. If that was the original point of the saying, then Luke's parallel to Matt. 5:32 exposed the Q version of Mark's reworked saying. The original would then have been, "Every one who divorces his wife and marries another commits adultery, and he who marries a woman divorced from her husband commits adultery" (Luke 16:18). This would be perfectly in keeping with Jesus' vision of the Kingdom without sexuality. It was permissible to dissolve marriage since the Kingdom would have no marriages. If, however, divorce took place only for the sake of remarriage, then the action had no relation to the future state of the Kingdom and was merely the continuation of the exercise of sexuality that characterized the world without knowledge of the future Kingdom.

The other issue is divorce itself, apart from the question of remarriage. Matthew probably gave the question the turn he did to contrast Jesus' teaching with rabbinic teaching on grounds for divorce.[56] He was encouraged in this by Mark, who put Jesus' pronouncement on remarriage into the setting of a discussion about divorce which was probably mostly Mark's creation. The saying on remarriage obviously assumed the availability of divorce. The commandment of the Lord against divorce in I Cor. 7:10–11 cannot be used to establish the originality of the divorce motif since it moved in the same Hellenistic context of a wife divorcing a husband as does Mark 10:12.

Jesus' view of a future Kingdom without sexuality and marriage explains his attitude toward family obligations as well. Luke's version was probably original. With the editorial addition removed, it reads: "There is no man who has left house or wife or brothers or parents or children, for the sake of the kingdom of God, who will not receive manifold." (Luke 18:29–30; Mark 10:29–30; Matt. 19:29.)[57]

Jesus' indifference to his own family sprang from the same vision of the Kingdom. Where there was no sexuality or marriage, there was no family. If, as I take it, Mark 3:34 was original and v. 35 secondary, Jesus replaced the concept of family with that of Kingdom.[58] "And looking around on those who sat about him, he said, 'Here are my mother and my brothers!' " The crowd who accepted his message of the Kingdom had prior claim over family because they would occupy the everlasting Kingdom, where family relationships count for nothing.

It might be possible to conclude from Jesus' teaching on sexuality that he was consistently negative in his attitude toward the bodily aspects of life in this world. This was not the case since in his vision of the Kingdom eating and drinking were perhaps the primary form of celebration of life in the new age. We have already noticed that the banquet was the form in which Jesus saw the Gentiles included in the blessings of the Kingdom (Matt. 8:11; Luke 13:29). This banqueting in the Kingdom explains the importance of Jesus' table fellowship during his ministry as well as the eschatological setting of the Lord's Supper. Jesus' eating with those who were prepared for the Kingdom was a preview and foretaste of life in the Kingdom. The vow of abstinence at the Lord's Supper assumed the resumption of eating and drinking in the Kingdom (Mark 14:25; Luke 22:16, 18).[59]

Jesus' general acceptance of the world and its natural processes, apart from sexuality, is confirmed by his use of nature in his parables. He could find in nature illustrations of the Kingdom because nature was the good creation of the King of the Kingdom. God's reign in the present natural world was a parable of his final complete reign in the world to come. The elimination of sexuality from the next world was, apparently, the one place where the dualistic temper of the times most strongly influenced Jesus' vision of reality. Perhaps the elimination of sexuality was only a logical deduction from the idea of a Kingdom adequately populated by the elect with no further need for reproduction.

Jesus' vision of the future Kingdom explains his teaching on politics as it has his teaching on sexuality. Only in this case, the situation was reversed. Instead of eliminating politics, the future Kingdom of God would have its own politics which would make the politics of the present world obsolete. Jesus' vision of the future was highly political. It was the vision of a theocracy. All other political systems were man-made and temporary. God would set up the final theocracy and it would endure forever. Therefore, all earthly political action had nothing to do with the Kingdom.

As Professor Cullmann has shown better than anyone heretofore, Jesus' teaching in relation to politics was predominantly a polemic against Zealot programs of direct political action.[60] So the saying about "the things that are Caesar's" and "the things that are God's" (Mark 12:17; Matt. 22:21; Luke 20:25) was intended to fend off such action so as not to grant to any Jewish political program some kind of equality with the future state of the Kingdom of God. On the other hand, with regard to the existing Roman state, that state also was not condoned. The saying was ironical and conceded to Caesar only what had no value for the Kingdom, namely, money for taxes. Because this was all the state deserved, it did not compete with the claims of the Kingdom. Since the times of this world and of Caesar were so brief in Jesus' view, Caesar could be tolerated. Besides, it was God's business to remove the states of this world. It would have been presumptuous for any man to usurp this kind of divine prerogative. The Kingdom was to be given, therefore man's only responsibility was to prepare to receive it.

Illustrations of the determining influence of Jesus' vision of the Kingdom upon his ethical teaching could be multiplied. The space of this chapter allows only one more example. The eschatological prophet also dealt with questions of the Law from the perspective of the Kingdom and its nearness. Matthew was correct in interpreting Jesus' teaching as fulfillment rather than abrogation of Law. The Law would be fulfilled in the Kingdom of God because there conditions would permit the complete realization of the will of God. Much of Law was an adjustment of the will of God to a continuing world whose circumstances simply did not allow the fulfillment of God's will. Whether or not Jesus said it, this explains the meaning of the provisions Moses made for divorce because of "hardness of heart" (Mark 10:5; Matt. 19:8). "Hardness of heart" stood for the continuing condition of a world unredeemed by the final, all-powerful action of God. In a continuing world, Law must take account of the circumstances of that world. This was what accommodation to "hardness of heart" meant. In contrast to Moses, Jesus was working out of a vision of a world unencumbered by "hardness of heart." The contrast between Jesus and his Jewish contemporaries was not the contrast between Law and Gospel or between merit and grace. The real contrast was between the perspective of Jews who needed to take the continuing world into account and the eschatological prophet who mainly took account of the world to come. There was no basic contradiction between Jesus and Moses. Each interpreted the will of God in concert with what each considered the prevailing conditions under which the people of God were to live out that will.

Jesus' choice of the summary of the Law is a perfect example of his acceptance of Law as the appropriate form of the will of God and his interpretation of it in accord with his eschatology. The saying of Jesus on the chief commandment appears in the forms of scholastic discussion and of controversy, which forms are products of the church and reflect its own debates. But these could well preserve the original teachings of Jesus although they come to us in churchly compositions.[61] The first commandment follows from the recognition that the Kingdom of God will be just that—the place where God will actually reign as the fountain of all good without any competing evil. The second commandment is a recognition of the Kingdom as the place where God will effect the complete well-being of man. So to love God and man is to recognize and live out already what will fundamentally characterize the future Kingdom.

Now it remains only to take this Christology of the eschatological prophet and his way of doing ethics and to discover its relevance for the modern world.

NOTES

1. Convenient descriptions of the eschatological prophet may be found in: H. M. Teeple, *The Mosaic Eschatological Prophet*, Journal of Biblical Literature Monograph Series, Vol. X (Philadelphia: Society of Biblical Literature, 1957); Oscar Cullmann, *The Christology of the New Testament*, tr. by Shirley C. Guthrie and Charles A. M. Hall (The Westminster Press, 1959), pp. 13–50; Rudolf Meyer, art. *"prophētēs," Theologisches Wörterbuch zum Neuen Testament*, ed. by G. Kittel, VI, pp. 826–828; Paul Volz, *Die Eschatologie der jüdischen Gemeinde im neutestamentlichen Zeitalter* (Tübingen: J. C. B. Mohr, 1934), pp. 193–194.

2. James Muilenburg, in *The Interpreter's Bible* (Abingdon Press, 1956), Vol. 5, p. 709. Von Rad finds this prophet only in Malachi (*Old Testament Theology*, tr. by D. M. G. Stalker, Vol. II, p. 289; Harper & Row, Publishers, Inc., 1965).

3. James Muilenburg against von Rad and Noth, "The Office of the Prophet in Ancient Israel," *The Bible in Modern Scholarship*, ed. by J. Philip Hyatt (Abingdon Press, 1965), p. 88.

4. Volz, *op. cit.*, pp. 194–195.

5. 4 Q Testimonia 5–8.

6. 11 Q Melch, ed. by A. S. Van Der Woude, "Melchisedek als himmlische Erlösergestalt in den neugefundenen eschatologischen Midrashim aus Qumran Höhle XI," *Oudtestamentische Studien* XIV (1956), pp. 354–373.

7. Josephus, *War* vii. 437 ff.

8. Josephus, *Antiquities* xviii. 5. 2.

9. Cf. G. Fohrer, *Die symbolische Handlungen der Propheten* (Zürich: Zwingli-Verlag, 1953); C. H. Dodd, "Jesus as Teacher and Prophet," *Mysterium Christi,* ed. by G. K. A. Bell and Adolf Deissman (Longmans, Green & Co., Inc., 1930), pp. 59, 60, 64, 65.

10. Cullmann, *op. cit.,* p. 117.

11. Rudolf Bultmann, *The History of the Synoptic Tradition,* tr. by J. Marsh (Harper & Row, Publishers, Inc., 1963), p. 257; K. L. Schmidt, *Der Rahmen der Geschichte Jesu* (Berlin: Tronitzsch, 1919), p. 216; and Willi Marxsen, *Der Evangelist Markus* (Göttingen: Vandenhoeck & Ruprecht, 1959), pp. 44, 45, consider the geography came with the pericope and is not the work of Mark. Bultmann considers the whole piece a legend of faith in the Messiahship of Jesus coupled with a Hellenistic polemic against the Jewish-Christian point of view represented by Peter. This classification obscures any historical event beneath the legend but does not rule out the possibility of such an event.

12. Reginald H. Fuller, *The Foundations of New Testament Christology* (Charles Scribner's Sons, 1965), p. 109.

13. Bultmann, *op. cit.,* pp. 283, 284.

14. Ernst Käsemann, "The Problem of the Historical Jesus," in *Essays on New Testament Themes,* tr. by W. J. Montague (Alec R. Allenson, Inc., 1964), p. 40.

15. Günther Bornkamm, *Jesus of Nazareth,* tr. by Irene and Fraser McLuskey with James M. Robinson (Harper & Brothers, 1961), p. 62.

16. Käsemann, *op. cit.,* p. 44. Cf. Norman Perrin, *Rediscovering the Teachings of Jesus* (Harper & Row, Publishers, Inc., 1967), p. 39.

17. Bornkamm: "He is in no way completely contained in this category, and differs from the customary ways of a

prophet." (*Op. cit.*, p. 56.) Käsemann: "It is thus very tempting to call him a prophet. But this will not do at all. No prophet could remove himself from the jurisdiction of Moses. . . . No prophet could be credited with the eschatological significance which Jesus obviously ascribed to his actions." (*Op. cit.*, p. 42.) Cullmann: " 'The Prophet of the end time' failed to include the activity of the 'living' Christ after Easter, although, it was just this . . . which was *the* fundamental Christological experience of the early Church." (*Op. cit.*, p. 48.)

18. Cullmann, *op. cit.*, p. 49.

19. Ernst Käsemann, *Exegetische Versuche und Besinnungen*, zweiter Band (Göttingen: Vandenhoeck & Ruprecht, 1964), p. 56.

20. Georg Strecker, "Zum Problem des Judenchristentums," in Walter Bauer, *Rechtgläubigkeit und Ketzerei in ältesten Christentum* (Tübingen: J. C. B. Mohr, 1964), pp. 252, 260, 286, 287.

21. Shlomo Pines, *op. cit.*

22. *Ibid.*, p. 14.

23. *Ibid.*, p. 15.

24. *Ibid.*, pp. 16, 17.

25. Louis Ginzberg, *The Legends of the Jews* (The Jewish Publication Society of America, 1959), Vol. IV, pp. 195 ff.

26. Ferdinand Hahn, *Christologische Hoheitstitel*, zweite Auflage (Göttingen: Vandenhoeck & Ruprecht, 1964), pp. 390 ff.

27. Bultmann, *op. cit.*, pp. 247, 248.

28. *Ibid.*, p. 108.

29. It is not important to look for the significance of the dove in the history of religions. It merely is a metaphor that signifies the manner of the Spirit's coming.

30. *Epi tēs gēs.*

31. For the eschatological significance of the booths, see Ernst Lohmeyer, "Die Verklärung Jesu nach den Markus-Evangelium," *Zeitschrift für die neutestamentliche Wissenschaft*, Vol. 21 (1922), pp. 194 ff.

32. Cf. Hahn, *op. cit.*, p. 339, and H. Baltensweiler, *Die Verklärung Jesu* (Zürich: Zwingli-Verlag, 1959).

33. Hahn, *op. cit.*, pp. 337, 338.

34. Bultmann, *op. cit.*, p. 35. For literature, see the addition to n. 4 on p. 388.

35. Hans Conzelmann, *The Theology of St. Luke*, tr. by Geoffrey Buswell (Harper & Row, Publishers, Inc., 1961), p. 139.

36. Conzelmann, *op. cit.*, p. 166.

37. Cf. Cullmann, *op. cit.*, pp. 28–30.

38. Volz, *op. cit.*, p. 167; Philipp Vielhauer, "Gottesreich und Menschensohn in der Verkündigung Jesu," in *Festschrift für Günther Dehn*, ed. by W. Schneemelcher (Neukirchen: Verlag der Buchhandlung des Erziehungsvereins, 1957), p. 77.

39. Hans Conzelmann, "Reich Gottes im Judentum und NT," in *Die Religion in Geschichte und Gegenwart*, 3d ed., Vol. V, pp. 914 ff.

40. Werner G. Kümmel, *Promise and Fulfilment* (London: SCM Press, Ltd., 1961), and Norman Perrin, *The Kingdom of God in the Teaching of Jesus* (The Westminster Press, 1963). Both authors climax their discussions of the Kingdom in Jesus' teaching with a description of the tension between the Kingdom as present and the Kingdom as future.

41. For our purposes we may disregard Luke's special doctrine of the binding of Satan between the temptation and the passion of Jesus. (Conzelmann, *The Theology of St. Luke*, p. 180.) Late Jewish eschatology expected Satan to be bound at the end. (Kümmel, *op. cit.*, p. 109; *Assumption of Moses* 10:1; W. Grundmann, art. *"iskuō," Theologisches Wörterbuch zum Neuen Testament*, III, pp. 403–404.)

42. Joachim Jeremias, *Jesus' Promise to the Nations*, tr. by S. H. Hooke (London: SCM Press, Ltd., 1958). "The incorporation of the Gentiles in the Kingdom of God, promised by the prophets, was expected and announced by Jesus as God's *eschatological act of power, as the great manifestation of God's free grace*." (P. 70.) For the same idea in Jewish eschatology, see Volz, *op. cit.*, pp. 171 f.

43. Joachim Jeremias, *The Parables of the Kingdom*, tr. by S. H. Hooke (Charles Scribner's Sons, 1963), p. 149.

44. The simple refusal to give any sign in Mark 8:12 with no mention of Jonah may be the more original form of the saying.

In either case the request for a sign would show an appreciation of the apparent incongruity between Jesus' activity and the Kingdom of God of the world to come. (Bultmann, *op. cit.*, pp. 117, 118.)

45. For the references in late Jewish literature, see Volz, *op. cit.*, pp. 165–173.

46. Walter Bauer, *A Greek-English Lexicon of the New Testament and Other Early Christian Literature*, rev. and ed. by William F. Arndt and F. Wilbur Gingrich (The University of Chicago Press, 1957), p. 212. For the literature of debate between realized and futurist eschatology, see Kümmel, *op. cit.*, pp. 19 ff., and Perrin, *The Kingdom of God in the Teaching of Jesus*, pp. 64 ff.

47. Bultmann, *op. cit.*, pp. 123, 401, 402.

48. Jeremias, *The Parables of the Kingdom*, p. 119.

49. Bultmann, *op. cit.*, p. 26.

50. Vielhauer, *loc. cit.*, pp. 51–79.

51. Jeremias, *The Parables of the Kingdom*, p. 49.

52. Bultmann, *op. cit.*, p. 26.

53. Ernst Lohmeyer, *Das Evangelium des Markus* (Göttingen: Vandenhoeck & Ruprecht, 1954), p. 257. Wilfred L. Knox recognizes Luke's version to be independent of Mark, *The Sources of the Synoptic Gospels*, ed. by H. Chadwick (London: Cambridge University Press, 1953), Vol. I, p. 90. Schweizer's unwillingness to attribute Mark 12:25 to Jesus rests on his unwillingness to place Jesus in a conversation between "pharisaic and apocalyptic minded Jews"—especially when the result associates Jesus with the apocalyptists. (Eduard Schweizer, *Das Evangelium nach Markus*, Das Neue Testament Deutsch, Vol. I, p. 140; Göttingen: Vandenhoeck & Ruprecht, 1967.) The position attributed to Jesus here is quite in keeping with other sayings on sexuality.

54. Bultmann recognizes Matt. 19:12 as a logion (*op. cit.*, pp. 26, 76).

55. *Ibid.*, p. 26; Schweizer, *op. cit.*, p. 144.

56. Bultmann, *op. cit.*, p. 27; Krister Stendahl, "Matthew," in *Peake's Commentary on the Bible*, ed. by Matthew Black and H. H. Rowley (Edinburgh: Thomas Nelson & Sons Ltd., 1962), p. 776.

57. Bultmann, *op. cit.,* pp. 110–111.

58. With Martin Dibelius, *From Tradition to Gospel,* tr. by B. L. Woolf (Charles Scribner's Sons, 1933), p. 57.

59. Joachim Jeremias, *The Eucharistic Words of Jesus,* tr. by Arnold Ehrhardt (The Macmillan Company, 1955), pp. 165 ff.

60. Oscar Cullmann, *The State in the New Testament* (Charles Scribner's Sons, 1956), pp. 20 f.

61. Bultmann, *op. cit.,* pp. 22 f., 146 f.

V

THE ESCHATOLOGICAL PROPHET
AND THE DAWN OF THIS WORLD

The good news for today is that we do not have to believe the same doctrines the New Testament authors believed or the same doctrines tradition has preserved as orthodoxy. It is one of the ironies of our time that bishops and doctors of the church attract most attention and enthusiasm not when they reaffirm tradition but when they publicly question it. This, I think is the main lesson to be learned from the phenomenal interest in Bonhoeffer, Bishop Robinson, and the no-God theologians; namely, traditional Christianity is impossible to believe for a large proportion of men in the Western world and, consequently, we are vastly relieved when important figures within the church give signs that they recognize this fact.

The positive side of this good news is that the man who cannot believe tradition need not sever connections with Christianity and the church. Although he died before he found it, Bonhoeffer was confident that there was a way for modern man to believe. Bishop Robinson has made some tentative suggestions for modifying traditional doctrines so that they may express convictions of men today. The no-God theologians announced the death of God, not to destroy religion, but to clear the way for a renaissance of faith. This chapter shares the hope of all these men and seeks to be helpful in the way they sought to be. What follows is an attempt to develop expressions of belief that differ enough from tradition to be believable but that are similar enough to be faithful. Our objective is to demonstrate one way to generate forms of religious conviction that are faithful both to tradition and to modern ways of thinking. The hope is to remain both Christian and sane. The good news is that this is possible.

Jesus of Nazareth opens up this possibility. He was obviously important to the earliest tradition. From a modern point of view it is equally obvious that this person really lived, that he qualifies as a historical reality. The historical Jesus then is a figure that both tradition and the modern mind recognize as real. Herein lies the possibility of bridging the rapidly widening gulf between the world of tradition and the modern world.

We must not expect too much from any particular alternative to tradition. The one we shall develop does not pretend to be the new Christianity for all men of our time. Its claims are more modest. It only hopes to be a viable alternative for a pocket of people who happen to share the convictional structure we shall describe and who are interested in having their religious convictions in a form congenial to this structure. Compared to the total membership of churches in the West, this proportion may be very small indeed.

The number of people who might actually avail themselves of this alternative to tradition is not so important as it might have been in times past. We proceed on the assumption that Western culture is fragmented now, composed of pockets of people, each pocket operating with its own consensus about reality and its own set of crucial issues. People in the church naturally share this variety of perspective with the result that we can no more look for unanimity inside the church than we can outside. Instead we must find a new church alive with alternative forms of faith. This church of the future must be a community with the grace to accept the kind of variety of opinion and action that would simply demolish any idea of community in a more homogeneous cultural situation.

What we are offering is one way of responding to tradition that produces one particular form of faith. It does not intend to exclude other ways of responding to tradition or other forms of faith. This way of responding to tradition is relatively logical and pragmatic. Certainly there are other ways of responding appropriately to more intuitive or idealistic turns of mind. Others might wish to leave to mystery some of the issues we prefer to examine. Every man in every cultural pocket must feel free to follow his own map of reality as he responds to tradition.

This tolerance for variety, of course, is more difficult to manage than to describe, especially for those of us who were nurtured and educated in what we thought was a homogeneous culture. Particularistic and exclusivistic attitudes learned in formative years are very difficult to exorcise later on. The difficulty seems compounded for those of us who are religious. Experience shows that whatever beautiful fruit religion may produce, there is an almost overwhelming tendency among religious people toward censoriousness. Perhaps Gamaliel's advice is still to the point. It was he who advised patience with new religious forms lest by opposing them, "you might even be found opposing God!" (Acts 5:39). If we can be sufficiently patient and accepting of one another, the new standards of orthodoxy will eventually emerge.

Given the rapid rate of cultural change, there is every probability that future Christianity will need to accept forms undreamed of now. But this required acceptance cuts both ways. We cannot resolve the tension between generations by dismissing the young people as infantile, any more than we can by exiling the elderly as people whom the times have passed by. We must move beyond such outworn polarities and learn to see one another in the church, not simply as young or old, believers or unbelievers, safe or dangerous, but as those who affirm tradition in usual ways compared to those who affirm tradition to unusual fashions.

Basic to our proposal is the contention that the secular gives form to the sacred; that is, ordinary experiences provide the conceptual forms that shape relatively amorphous religious experiences. In the Judeo-Christian tradition, the movement from secular to sacred is clearest perhaps in the doctrine of God. This tradition starts out by intimating that its God, unlike other gods, cannot be identified with any particular form. "You shall not make for yourself a graven image, or any likeness of anything that is in heaven above, or that is in the earth beneath, or that is in the water under the earth; you shall not bow down to them or serve them." Even though it was necessary to conceive of God in some way, Moses commanded that God could not be *defined* this way. To protect further the mystery of God, no Israelite was permitted to see him. Nevertheless, right in the midst of the mystery, the people of Israel developed a doctrine of God as a particular king. What happened was that they surveyed their cultural situation for the most exalted figure in their universe, the Oriental king, and made him the first model for their doctrine of God. Then, as experience with this God concept accumulated, other models from secular life were explored. This was no contradiction of the commandment. They had to have *some* way of conceiving God. The commandment meant that no particular way could be the final way. Jesus, for example, continued the doctrine of God as king but preferred to complement it with the model of father which was also in the tradition. The added tone of father tempered the austerity and severity of God as king. Father was more adequate to experiences of sympathy and intimacy than king. In this way, secular experiences continued to provide the forms that gave order and meaning to sacred experiences.

In the Biblical period, there was no distinction between the secular and the sacred in the modern sense. All phenomena in the Bible were capable of religious interpretation because, in that culture, all of life was open to the influences of heaven. The distinction between secular and sacred arose when modern science began to make sense of some events independent of heavenly influences. The phenomena that could continue to receive their explanation from heaven belonged to the sacred realm. The phenomena more comfortably explained in terms of this world produced a secular realm.

The rise of an autonomous secular realm was a challenge and a threat to religion, because it seemed as if the sacred realm lost whatever ground the secular realm gained. The majority of the church was unprepared for this apparent attack. It had been so long since Christians had needed to discover forms in common life to shape their religious experience that they had forgotten it had ever been necessary. Orthodoxy was so accustomed to its particular combination of religion and culture that it had long since granted the cultural factor the status of special revelation. Consequently, Christendom's accommodation to culture was not really open to review, much less to redoing.

This failure of Western orthodoxy to recognize its own cultural relativity is what threatens traditional Christianity with obsolescence today. The remedy is obvious. Western Christianity must admit the relativity of its dearest formulations and return to common life to discover new and lively shapes.

If this is a correct assessment of Western Christianity's predicament, no one ought to be surprised when the new formulations turn out to be startlingly different from conventional ones. After all, the cardinal formulations of orthodoxy have been out of touch with the movement of culture for so long that the accumulated lag is fairly massive. The trip that Christians at home in tradition must now take is of the same dimensions as the trip of the astronauts to the moon. Accordingly they should expect some loss of orientation en route and a measure of discomfort in their new environment. Once we realize the cultural relativity of traditional formulations, the next step is to devise some means to expose the contrast between that culture which shaped orthodoxy and the culture of today. Once the cultural context is exposed, the reshaping of doctrine called for by modern secular culture will unfold almost by itself.

The device I have chosen to expose the cultural gap between

the era of tradition and the secular era is what Willem Zuurdeeg called convictional structure.[1] As I use that term, I mean
a set of prereligious convictions about man's total environment
and his relation to it that provide the working basis for the life
of any particular culture. I have chosen this term because it is
flexible enough to include the scope and intensity of the attitudes and commitments in any culture that are fundamental to
its religious formulations. Available descriptions of the cultural
gap between traditional Christianity and the secular age suffer
mainly from narrowness of scope. Programs to translate Biblical
thought into contemporary idioms that depend on Heidegger,
linguistic analysis, or Lutheran tradition all give too private a
view of the human situation.[2] Sociologists of religion are better
guides in terms of scope. Harvey Cox is especially useful here,
but he is strangly shy with the Bible.[3] He seems unaware that
it is as heavily conditioned by its cultural context as the new
secular Christianity must be. Van Harvey is an excellent guide
to the respect for history essential to a viable secular equivalent
to tradition.[4]

There are two possible ways to get at the convictional structures of ancient and modern cultures that underlie their religious formulations. We shall prefer the selective style of a
Hercule Poirot to the vacuum cleaner approach of a Sherlock
Holmes. The convictional structures basic to the religious forms
of the secular man in our illustration and to traditional religion
show their essential contours in response to only five questions.
Who controls history? Is reality fixed or in process of becoming? Where is primary reality? Is man able to cope with his own
situation? What is the major consideration in the formation of
ethics? A comparison of the answers that each convictional
structure gives prepares the way for the form of religion that
each convictional structure requires.

Who controls history? Traditional culture would tend to explain history as the fateful product of some extrahistorical
agency. Secular man would explain history as man's own proj-

ect. Traditional man would say God controls history. Secular man would say man does.

Is reality fixed or in process of becoming? The posture of the God of tradition symbolizes its answer: He is enthroned, sedentary, eternally the same. And from eternity he has fixed the pattern of what the universe will become. In his own good time he will put an end to this changeable world, conform it to its eternal prototype, and fix it in its perfect form forever. The similarity to Platonic ideas is obvious. Secular man, on the contrary, views reality as a process of continual change. It is inconceivable to the secular man we are describing that the universe ever had a literal beginning or that it will have a literal end. As far as he can judge, it always has been adapting and adjusting and will continue to do so. He does not attempt to chart the process with an upward or downward slope or spiral. He accepts process as it is and works in it. If the process is to slope or spiral, improve or deteriorate, it will be man who nudges it that way within the limits of the possibilities open to him.

The question about the locus of reality is a companion to the question about the mobility of reality. Where is primary reality? For the man of tradition, primary, archetypal reality is in heaven. For secular man, the only place he knows for reality is here in the universe.

The last two questions probe more deeply into the life-style than the first three. Is man able to cope with his own situation? The contrast between answers here is fairly stark. The man of tradition says no. The powers that impinge on man are too overwhelming for him. This is sad because these powers press man into tragedy. By contrast, the secular man has more confidence in his ability to cope with his situation. To be sure, many aspects of his situation are set by environment and previous history. Still he sees open to man an important range of possibilities and feels that man is developing an increasing capacity to cope with his environment and his past. He also knows that he is free to be foolish in the exercise of this expanding capacity.

Finally, there is the matter of ethics. What is the major consideration in the formation of ethics? What determines the evaluation of conduct as good or bad, to be desired or to be avoided? For the man at home in tradition, there is a revealed pattern of conduct that all men are obligated to accept and follow. The man at home in this world sees the matter quite differently. He chooses the shape of his ethics in accordance with the vision of the future he hopes to bring. His ethics is a combination of the strategy and tactics he devises to bring that future into reality together with the style of life that enjoys whatever measure of that future is already available. His private ethic is worked out in concert with the groups to which he belongs; that is, in the light of the aims of those groups and the means they have chosen to achieve and to enjoy their accomplishments.

It is clear from these answers to common questions that the convictional structures represented are quite different. It is also clear that if the convictional structure of secular culture is used to shape religion, the result will differ significantly from traditional religion. To illustrate this difference, we shall turn to specific aspects of the message of Jesus. But first, another side of the hermeneutic we are illustrating needs explanation.

It is already obvious that our approach to tradition provides for significant difference. What about significant similarity or, which is more to the point, continuity? This must be provided for since upon it depends the right to continue to be called Christian. It is the special advantage of our hermeneutical method that it provides for both differences from and continuity with Jesus' message and traditional Christianity. Accordingly, I have chosen to call this approach a hermeneutic of analogy. This means that it aims at a relationship of analogy between traditional theology and secular theology. What is special about a relationship of analogy is its inclusion of differences and similarities. Differences make it possible to accommodate as many cultural strains as a pluralistic society may require. Similarity preserves the continuity with tradition that makes the result a faithful equivalent of tradition. In order to provide for the cultural variety that marks our time, we must cease to expect exact equivalents to tradition. Analogical equivalents to traditional Christianity are the appropriate results to work for in a pluralistic society like our own.

For continuity with orthodoxy and faithfulness to tradition, the key element in the relation of analogy is "similarity." It will be fair to ask secular equivalents to traditional Christianity whether they conserve, distort, or simply lose important elements in tradition. I shall claim that the important elements in tradition to conserve are the uniqueness of Jesus, the most exalted role conceivable for God, and a program for the spread of the love of God in private and public life in our time comparable to the Kingdom of God that Jesus proclaimed for his time. This last element, the spread of the love of God, is, as we shall see, more a matter of continuity of direction than repetition of a particular program. Any program designed for a specific cultural situation is too bound to that situation to be transferable to another. However, it is possible to detect the aim in Jesus' proclamation and imagine a program that has the same aims for the secular situation—a program that would move history in the same direction as it moved in Jesus' vision.

The secular convictional structure or set of operational assumptions about reality has already influenced the discussion. We chose Jesus of Nazareth as a focus of faith instead of the risen Christ because Jesus is the kind of reality this view can credit. It simply cannot see the risen, spiritual Christ of the traditional resurrection appearances because such a being is off this map of reality. It is not a matter of belief or unbelief. It is a matter of sense versus nonsense. A person with the secular convictional pattern under consideration finds it inconceivable that a dead man be made alive again by the power of God. Either the man in question was not really dead or he is "alive again" in some nonliteral sense. This is not to dispute that such an event happened for the earliest witnesses to the resurrection.

They saw what they said they saw. They must be permitted the experience of their own convictional structure. But the convictional structure with which we are working does not permit the same experience.

We have run up against the first apparent impasse between the traditional convictional structure and the convictional structure of our illustration. From the point of view of tradition, we are confronted with a striking difference. But a hermeneutic of analogy has prepared us for this eventuality. Instead of being stunned we are led on to inquire where precisely the difference in convictional structures lies that has produced this apparent impasse of religious convictions. We shall see that resurrection is an especially fruitful place to have begun since it focuses attention upon the differences between religious forms based on the traditional convictional structure and religious forms based on the modern view of reality with which we are working.

The resurrection of Jesus is inconceivable to the man in our illustration primarily because his view of reality does not permit this kind of action in history. In fact, he is only able to participate in the modern world by carefully excluding this kind of possibility. Events must be explained by powers within history and nature. Only by strict adherence to this view of agency in history and nature has it been possible to produce the benefits of modern science and technology. Only by removing the space for "God" on the data sheet has it been possible to carry out the experiments and draw the conclusions that are the basis for modern life. So long as men supposed that God might intrude into the experiments, no settled conclusion could be drawn.

This is nothing against God. It is important to emphasize that the decision to exclude God's direct agency from the process of nature was not a religious decision. It had no necessary connection with belief in or rejection of the existence of God. It becomes a religious decision only in the derivative sense that it implies that it cannot be that God does that kind of thing. This may seem shocking until we recall the source for the tra-

ditional view of God. The idea of a God with unlimited power
to effect whatever he wished in nature and history came from
the first century's way of looking at reality. In that culture,
nature and history were understood as pawns of heavenly
powers that determined what had to happen. The early church
understood God's relation to the world in the same way. He was
distinguished from the other claimants to mastery over the
world mainly by his superior power. Out of this convictional
structure came the traditional idea of the omnipotent God—a
God of unlimited power. This view found models for God in
Oriental and Hellenistic kings. Now that this whole way of
looking at agency in nature and history has become obsolete,
the doctrine of an omnipotent God as the final explanation of
effective agency in this world has as little cogency as the col-
umn on astrology in some daily newspapers.

Again I insist this is not to malign God. It simply means that
he must be related to nature and history in some other fashion
than as a super Oriental or Hellenistic potentate used to relate
to his realm. Again we find that the religious conviction depends on prereligious or extrareligious convictions. When convictions about reality in general change, religious convictions
change.

To bring a doctrine of God into conformity with modern convictions requires that God be related to the world by suasion
rather than by a direct exercise of power. The power will have
to reside where the convictional structure specifies: in the
forces of nature and in the agency of man. God's role is to persuade man to use his agency in history in the way that he indicated in the career of Jesus of Nazareth. That, I submit,
would be the beginning of an analogous equivalent to the traditional Christian doctrine of God in the convictional structure
of our illustration.

I admit that a God with limited power, related to history
only by suasion, is strikingly different from the omnipotent God
of the Bible who does whatever on earth he pleases. A hermeneutic of analogy is not put off by this. It stays to ask about the

possibility of underlying analogical correspondence. I contend that such correspondence is present here. The trick is to approach both convictional structures from an angle that reveals the important similarity.

I suggest that the illuminating angle is the comparison of roles for God in the convictional structures. Who is "God" in the traditional convictional structure? He is the most important person, the one with the most decisive influence on the course of the world that convictional structure could conceive. Accordingly, God was conceived and experienced by the church in terms of unlimited power.

The convictional structure of our illustration would see its most important person in quite another way. Omnipotence is not available to anyone in the secular view of reality. Here the most important role for a transcendent person would be the persuasion of the effective agents in history of the wisdom and goodness of the *divine purpose* so that they would become heartily willing advocates and executors on earth of that purpose. By virtue of fulfilling the most important function conceivable in each convictional structure, a hermeneutic of analogy would claim that the two doctrines of God are similar in an important way and therefore that the newer view of God is analogous to the older view. Now we are prepared to return to the resurrection of Jesus to inquire after its analogous equivalent in the newer view.

The literal return of Jesus to life cannot have happened for the man in our illustration. He has not seen the resurrected Lord. He has not seen anyone alive after death. His convictional structure requires a consistent rejection of ghosts in order to make sense of all that may happen to him. By assuming this posture toward the phenomenon of death, he intends no offense against the Christian doctrine of Jesus' resurrection. It is not a religious decision. It implies nothing for or against God or Jesus. The traditional resurrection simply cannot happen in his view of reality. What then will he do with Jesus' resurrection?

He may do with it something like what we have seen in the Synoptic authors. He may use the resurrection as an invitation to see in some other experience of Jesus an acceptable occasion for faith. Our treatment of the resurrection stories in the Synoptics showed that they used the resurrection to point to Jesus' ministry. Mark saw that ministry as the first career of the Son of Man calling for a second career that would fulfill God's purpose for history. Matthew pointed to Jesus as the teacher of commands which, if obeyed, would lead to an experience of him as the decisive illustration of what God has in mind for man. Luke pointed beyond resurrection to Jesus as the fulfillment of Old Testament messianic prophecies and as the one who reveals himself in the celebration of the Lord's Supper. To repeat, the second-generation church found the original resurrection witness unconvincing until they turned to experiences of Jesus that were directly available to them. On this extraresurrection basis, they were able to affirm the original resurrection witness. Our illustration will follow this lead.

We have already turned to that Jesus of Nazareth in our own way as the eschatological prophet. What may this mean to the inquirer in our illustration who cannot affirm that Jesus literally rose from the dead? Again we meet a striking difference between the new and the old. And again we ask if there is not some analogous equivalent in the contemporary convictional structure to traditional resurrection. Assent to the resurrection in the Synoptic forms of faith had as its main Christological point the intention to affirm, along with the earliest church, that Jesus was the unique revelation of what God intended for man. The analogous conviction would be that on the basis of a historical investigation of the career of Jesus of Nazareth, he was the most important declaration of God's intention for man.

We find then that the resurrection in Matthew, Mark, and Luke invites the man in our illustration to see whether Jesus of Nazareth commends himself as the most important illustration of what man is intended to be. But what sense can he make of this eschatological prophet and his message in terms of a contemporary convictional structure?

In the original view, Jesus was literally alive. He lived in the other world and appeared occasionally to men in this world. Since the other world and its life after death have been removed, there is no way for the convictional structure in which we are working now to *conceive* of a way or a place for Jesus to continue to live literally after having died. It is not that our secular man is protesting against life after death. It is just that there is no conceptual possibility of it for him.

This does not mean that Jesus is not alive. Indeed, Jesus is very much alive for the person who believes that he is the last word on the destiny of man. But he is alive in the only way this secular view of reality permits persons of past history to be alive—in lively remembrance of history. The modern person who commits himself to the historical Jesus as the definition of the meaning of his life finds Jesus more alive to him and for him than any other person who happens to be his literal contemporary by virtue of the accident of birth.

This lively contact with the past through remembrance follows a great Biblical tradition that prevailed before there were other worlds and resurrections to them. Professor Childs has given one description of how memory actualized tradition when they occurred together in a context of faithful commitment.[5] Israel was related to the exodus in the same way secular Christians might relate to Jesus' resurrection.

Actualization is the process by which a past event is contemporized for a generation removed in time and space from the original event. When later Israel responded to the continuing imperative of her tradition through her memory, that moment in time likewise became an Exodus experience. Not in the sense that later Israel again crossed the Red Sea. This was an irreversible, once-for-all event. Rather, Israel entered the same redemptive reality of the Exodus generation.[6]

The redemptive quality of this lively relationship to the historical Jesus brings us to the third aspect of the analogous equivalent to primitive resurrection faith.

First, the resurrection of Jesus convinced the church of his uniqueness. Secondly, it convinced the church that he was alive. Finally, it mediated new life to Jesus' followers. We can say the same for those who follow the eschatological prophet in the lively relationship of historical memory. Once Jesus recommends himself as the last word on the meaning and direction of life, he resolves the confusion, ambiguity, and alienation that mark life apart from meaning and direction. In fact, to the man who sees meaning and direction as the major issues of existence, a decisive word about them means his salvation. The assurance that comes with a viable answer releases in him all his latent energies and capacities. He finds himself encouraged to commit himself to definite action and in the process finds his true self coming into being. In terms of the older view, he experiences the equivalent of rebirth or regeneration. It is as though he had been dead and is now alive.

Nothing essential to the primitive experience of the resurrection of Jesus is lost in the this-worldly, process view of the contemporary convictional structure. Each important feature of that experience finds an analogous equivalent. Resurrection leads to the historical Jesus. The historical Jesus becomes the eschatological prophet. The eschatological prophet leads to the eschatology of the Kingdom of God. The eschatology of the Kingdom of God leads to ethics.

We have said that the resurrection points to the eschatological prophet as the supreme illustration of what God intends man's destiny to be. This will mean finding the analogous equivalent to Jesus' message, eschatology, and ethics.

Jesus' Message

We have seen that the main burden of this prophet was to announce that the God of Israel would soon enter history and nature to conform them to the destiny he had appointed. This was to be an event like the resurrection, that is to say, some irresistible power would affect it from outside of history. This is just as inconceivable in the modern framework of our illustration as the resurrection.

Does Jesus' announcement of the *eschaton* have a modern analogous equivalent? Unless it does, faith in Jesus of Nazareth cannot even be an option. This is, in some ways, a more difficult question than the question about the analogous equivalent of resurrection. The resurrection happened in the life of the early church, but the announced arrival of the Kingdom of God did not.

There must be no softening of the difficulty or else the true thrust of Jesus' ministry is lost. Jesus promised the end of the world and it did not come. Does that promise have continuing importance although it did not and in our modern view cannot happen as he promised it? It is natural to want to conclude that his announcement of the end was all an unfortunate mistake and may be simply disregarded. This is what the vast majority of Protestant interpreters in effect suggest. But we have seen that there can be no honest appropriation of Jesus of Nazareth that disregards what was most important in his message. If Christians are able to affirm some finality for Jesus while disregarding his announcement of the end, it must be that they are grounding their convictions elsewhere than on the historical Jesus. When we are dealing with the historical figure, the eschatology is unavoidable. It would be no exaggeration to say that the historical Jesus did die rather than renounce or soften his eschatology.

As we noted in the last chapter, Jesus' program was summarized in the announcement, "The time is fulfilled, the kingdom of God is at hand; repent, and believe in the gospel." From a secular point of view, the most striking thing about this statement is its fateful perspective on history. It affirms not that some process native to history has come to flower of itself but rather that the time is ripe because of a decision made outside of history. The one who has made this decision intends to enter history, overpower it, and conform it to a prearranged pattern. Man's only role is to accept the inevitability of this pattern and prepare to enter it by conforming his personal relationships to it ahead of time. From a secular point of view such a proposal is, of course, impossible.

It is not a matter of not having faith. There is simply nothing there for a secular man to respond to. He cannot decide for this option as opposed to alternatives and turn in its direction, because Jesus' statement as it stands offers no live option at all. History just does not work that way for him. According to a secular convictional structure, history is the project of men and not of an outsider. Its course cannot be determined by a decision made outside of history.

It might be objected that the secular man ought at least to be able to pick out the goal indicated by the statement and decide for or against that regardless of the issue of agency in history. Again the incongruity between his convictional structure and the convictional structure behind the statement prevents him from recognizing a real option. Here the issue is the mobility of reality. In terms of the doctrine of the two ages, Jesus' announcement anticipates the arrival of a new age whose arrangements will be permanent and not subject to change. There is no such arrangement in a secular convictional structure where reality is in flux. So, in terms both of agency in history and the mobility of reality, the conflict of convictional structures prevents effective communication.

It is worth emphasizing again that the secular man's failure to respond to Jesus' message is no indication of his religious disposition. Often traditional Christians assume that a secular man must be an unbeliever when he fails to respond to their statements about Christianity. More often than not, the absence of response is a polite way of registering incomprehension. What is needed is to recast the traditional statement into the secular convictional structure. Then it may become a call for decision and action.

Adjusted for the autonomy of history and the flux of reality, the recast statement might look something like this: Given the vast opportunities for bringing misery or well-being upon the world today, it is high time that men choose the aim of history represented by Jesus' interpretation of "kingdom of God." So drop whatever other aims in history you have been pursuing and enlist all your energies in pursuit of these. If enough men respond, it could mean that mankind is on its way to an important improvement of its condition. That would be good news.

This recast message of Jesus results by asking how his eschatology functioned in his convictional structure. Let us run through the translation process again. Jesus' message served the purpose of declaring all that needed to be done to the world before it would fulfill the purpose of God. In other words, it described the ideal world in contrast to the world as it was. One could say that it functioned like a utopia. This function can be maintained in the convictional structure of our illustration once adjustments have been made for that structure.

We have already noted the problem of the agency of an all-powerful God in the primitive convictional structure in connection with resurrection. We substituted the role of suasion for the role of power. In connection with eschatology, we must specify who the new agents in history are that the suasive God intends to engage to arrange the destiny for the world that Jesus' eschatology defined. In the convictional structure of our illustration, there is only one agent for historical events analogous to the agency of the God of the traditional view. The agent is, of course, man with the startling difference that man's power is very limited. But limited as he is, history belongs to him in the measure that anything at all can be accomplished in it. In the view of our illustration, man assumes the direct historical agency which God had in the traditional view. It is God's role to persuade man how he is to use that agency. In the older view, man is waiting for God to arrange man's destiny. In the newer view, God is waiting for man.

There is one other startling difference between the two views. The other adjustment to the traditional eschatology has to do with the feasibility of Jesus' vision for the future. In the convictional structure of Jesus' message, the Kingdom of God would really happen. There was to be an end to the world as it had been, after which the Kingdom of God would break in completely and continue forever in unchanging perfection. Here the underlying difference between convictional structures is not so apparent as with agency in history. It is not now primarily a matter of a difference of degree between limited and unlimited power. It has to do with fundamentally different ways of viewing reality. In the older view, reality is ultimately static. God sits on his throne. This unchanging, sedentary God permits some variation in the course of nature and history but only within fixed limits. Thus history may be divided into epochs, each with a character of its own. The time of Israel and the time of the church of this age and the age to come, or the time before creation and the time after creation, or the time before the Fall and the time after the Fall. In the newer view, nature and history are a single process in continual flux. A beginning and end to the process are inconceivable. So far as this view can tell, the universe has always been and always will be. In this view, eschatology becomes more a matter of defining direction of effort than of defining final achievement.

This does not mean that no achievement of goals is anticipated. The ethics of this eschatology is a strategy and tactic for accomplishing whatever is possible. At the same time no particular achievement is mistaken for the fulfillment of a final design. Just as heaven is higher than the earth in the older view, so in the newer view the ends toward which the church works float out ahead of its grasp. Jesus' vision of the Kingdom informs the church of the direction which the process ought to take. As the responsible, effective agents of history, the church undertakes to move the process in that direction. It does not matter that you never arrive, because the process never arrives. The point is to encourage the proper movement.

Eschatology and Ethics

In the secular form of Christianity we are developing, God abdicates his traditional political role but not as a protest against politics. Rather, he steps down in order to make way for his adult sons to execute the kind of political program which in older views he promised to implement by himself. We call God's program a political program because it used politics as a model and declared a particular political goal. But it was more inclusive than most political programs. It sought to affect all areas of human life, individual and corporate.

The greatest heresy in orthodoxy has been to lose sight of the political aspect of Jesus' message and its full sociological scope. The church has been so preoccupied with programs for increasing personal virtue and piety that it has trivialized the range of the concerns that Jesus attributed to God. In effect, modern orthodoxy has replaced the Kingdom of God with private religious experiences and individual survival after death. In the secular world that we have defined, this is not even interesting, let alone exciting enough to call for commitment. Nor is it relevant enough to inform every facet of life.

From one point of view, the trivializing of Jesus' message is excusable. It is impossible to watch and pray unwaveringly for an event that has been coming any moment for nineteen hundred years. Some adjustment was necessary. What was tragic from a hermeneutical point of view was an adjustment of Jesus' hope that lost one of the most important things in it. Anyone who claims to follow Jesus today must retain the scope of his message.

One other characteristic of Jesus' vision of the coming Kingdom is as important as scope, namely, concreteness. Jesus' vision of the Kingdom of God had clear enough contours to provide guidance in the particular issues of life. In Jesus' Kingdom, the economic and religious outcasts of society would be granted full status, so Jesus made a point of associating with them. The Kingdom would eliminate illness and demon possession, so Jesus attacked these with healing and exorcism. The Kingdom was likely to judge men of exalted economic and religious status, so Jesus warned the wealthy and pious. When asked about the important commandment, Jesus' vision of the Kingdom highlighted the love of God and love of neighbor because God would reign there for man's highest good. After adjusting the Kingdom of God for man's autonomy in history and for the process character of reality, the resulting conception should not lack concreteness. Next to triviality, vagueness is the ranking heresy of orthodox equivalents to the Kingdom of God.

In the application of a secularized version of the Kingdom of God to the modern world, concreteness is achieved by transmuting the one grand fixed end of Jewish eschatology into a cluster of mobile ends. These ends in turn are ranked in a scale of relative priority depending upon opportunities for advancing toward the accomplishment of each one, and the urgency of the need in each case. This continually shifting list of priorities guides the individual and the church in the distribution of their energies. What is required is the opposite of the one-track mind.

For example, peace is the most pressing issue in the modern world from the point of view of Jesus' message. Nuclear weapons make possible the destruction of civilization as well as the destruction of the possibilities of realizing any of the aims of the Kingdom of God. However, war as a means of dealing with international conflict is not likely to be eliminated in the immediate future. Therefore, it is important now to concentrate on opposing the spread of nuclear weapons to more countries in order to lessen the probability of their use when threat of war occurs. But nuclear weapons have put war in a new light. War in any part of the world might lead to nuclear war, thus every war becomes the concern of every civilized person on earth. War can no longer be a local affair of the nations directly involved. It follows that some forum is required to focus world opinion against war as a means of handling national conflicts and to replace war with international police action where particular nations insist on war in spite of world opinion.

Something like the United Nations is obviously the forum required. Its effectiveness depends on the inclusion of all the nations of the world so that world opinion may be brought to bear most forcibly. This, of course, requires the inclusion of a nation like Communist China.

To make this forum effective as a means of preventing war, it is especially important that none of the powerful nations engage in war apart from the processes of this forum. To do so weakens the main hope civilization has of avoiding war. In the light of this consideration alone, the commitment of United States forces in Vietnam without United Nations sanction is contrary to the requirements of Jesus' message. Such action can only lead to cynicism among the nations of the world when the United States claims to follow a policy of peace, let alone when it claims the guidance of the God of Christianity for its national policy.

The point here has been to illustrate how concrete the vision of the Kingdom for our time must be if it is to reflect faithfully the original vision of Jesus.

The raising of the difficult problem of peace brings with it the question of the chances of a vision like the Kingdom ever coming to pass in the real world. It may fairly be asked whether this is a realistic hope. Christians are committed to hope by Jesus' vision whether it is achievable in the foreseeable future or not. But secular Christianity grounds its hope upon the new possibilities available to man rather than upon the arbitrary, irresistible intervention of God. Commitment to Jesus means commitment to hope, if only to keep alive the ideas of man's higher well-being contained in that hope. But hope has an even more effective role in the real world of actual possibilities. The stance of hope opens up possibilities that would not come to light without the climate of hope.

This power of hope to change history has already demonstrated itself in the case of slavery. The vision of Jesus condemned slavery but until the industrial revolution there was no way to eliminate slave labor and still maintain civilization as it was known. But the ideal of freedom from slavery was maintained with moral force by the vision of the Kingdom of God until the possibility of putting it into effect came to pass. The industrial revolution brought engines and machines as a possible alternative to slave power. At this point, the hope of emancipation became effective toward its realization. First, by the inspiring recognition that slavery was no longer an economic necessity and, secondly, by pressing for its elimination, a hope hitherto impossible of achievement became possible.

The same power of hope to open up new possibilities is operating now with regard to war. Until the emergence of modern technology, war could be justified as the necessary means to redistribute the scarce goods of nature required to sustain life. In an environment of scarcity, survival requires predatory action. The first scarce commodity is space. But with the emergence of the twin technologies of birth control and abortion, it is possible to adjust the population of the world to the living space available in the world. The second scarce commodity has been food. Here too there is grounds for hope. The increased knowledge and skill in production, preservation, and distribution of food provide the possibility of matching population growth with adequate food. The Christian can see these new technical possibilities as occasions to press for bringing the peace of Jesus' Kingdom nearer to the reality of this world.

But does the vision for the modern world analogous to Jesus' vision of the Kingdom of God take into account the greed and lust for power that tradition sees imbedded in human nature? Is not the traditional strategy closer to the hard realities when it calls for a remaking of human nature as the necessary precondition of any social revolution? From the point of view both of Jesus' vision and of its secular equivalent, the answer is no. Jesus did not call for or offer a new human nature as a condition of entering the Kingdom. He called for repentance which was a radical turning from the ends which men ordinarily pursue to the ends of the Kingdom of God. This implies that the problem is not located in man's nature but rather in the direction of his life commitment. In similar fashion, a secular theology sees man not so much ontologically defective as wrongly committed. His life is chaotic, confused, and harmful due to the ambiguity or cruelty of his commitments and his ambivalence toward the goals he does entertain for his life. Consequently, a secular theology of Jesus' message would see the best chances for personal and social integration and fulfillment in a commitment to a vision and program for the fulfillment of the God-appointed destiny of the world.

From the secular point of view, any other expectation for man in this world is hopeless. The means to remake man are simply not available. Nor do those who profess to follow the path of ontological renewal seem to operate very differently from those who follow the path of repentance. The secular theologian must be permitted the suspicion that "regeneration" or "new birth" are other cultural ways of describing the same process he calls repentance. Regeneration is Christianity's way of dealing with man in a culture that has lost all confidence in man. Repentance is Christianity's way of dealing with man in a culture that has retained a measure of confidence in him.

All this does not mean that a secular equivalent of hope minimizes the obstacles to change. The references to demons and Satan in Jesus' teaching must be allowed to have their full secular equivalent today. There are wasteful and chaotic forces in nature and history that must be reckoned with. Modern man's success in controlling or accommodating himself to nature has been phenomenal. Modern man's failure to direct history into humane channels has been almost as phenomenal. The hopeful side of this failure of man to be humane in modern times is that the secular perspective enables us to see that this failure has been man's own choice and not the imposition of fate. This realization frees us to see where and why man chooses foolishly and to concentrate our efforts to be persuasive accordingly. The secular perspective delivers us from ineffectual hand-wringing before supposedly insuperable mythical obstacles.

Whenever hope in history is suggested, the ghost of the social gospel haunts us with the outworn idea of inevitable progress. The secular world just as effectively debunks the fixed idea of inevitable disaster. From a secular point of view, one idea is as superstitious as the other. The only thing inevitable about history is decision. Men must decide the way history shall go.

Automation provides an illustration of another side of the relation of eschatology and ethics as they are adjusted to the modern world. In America, it is relatively easy to anticipate a social crisis when automation enables us to produce goods and services with much less time and effort than heretofore. When that time comes, economic achievement will no longer be an apt measure of a man or a society. This crisis in the value system of American society will provide an unusual opportunity for influencing that society's choice of a way of life. The eschatological Kingdom's vision of unlimited social justice and its concomitant, personal relationships of love, can guide the church to be ready with suggestions for this time. Meanwhile, its ethical energy should now be devoted to hammering out by trial and error a style of life that will be fully appropriate only when that time comes. This wrestling with a style of life for the future will tend to hasten its coming by demonstrating the superior opportunity for humanizing life that comes with emancipation from economic preoccupation. Also, the church should devise means to hasten automation in order that more people now living might have a chance at the new, fuller possibilities for life.

But this reading of signs for the future will include sobering signs of the society's fear of change that makes it anxiously cling to the familiar. This must be understood not simply as an evidence of selfish resistance to justice and love. Men and societies, like their counterparts in nature, are predominantly products of their past experiences. When faced with a new situation for which this past experience does not provide obvious direction, panic is to be expected as well as creative accommodation. When anxiety is coupled with the desire to keep the *status quo* on the part of those who have found it highly rewarding economically, we can easily understand the massive resistance that people who live out of the future are bound to meet among their fellows. Perhaps this experience would be the analogous equivalent of persecution in the life of the early church. However that may be, the church as a group that seriously takes up this analogy to Jesus' eschatology would be clearly distinguished from certain other groups in society that make their avowed purpose to perpetuate the past.

I do not wish to overemphasize the contrast between the past and the future. From the point of view of process, past and future blend into each other. There is never complete discontinuity. Every creative movement into the future builds upon and carries forward elements of the past.

Nor do I wish to confuse process with progress. There is no inevitability that the future will be an improvement over the past. Process only dictates that movement is inevitable and therefore that mankind is always choosing to enrich or impoverish his existence. One more observation will make our illustration of an analogous ethics extended enough to suggest how this modern analogy to the primitive form of eschatological ethics might unfold.

We have said that we must remain faithful to the full scope of the Kingdom in the message of Jesus. It is important that ethics unfold accordingly. Once responsibility for the execution of eschatology has been accepted, the communal scope of ethics comes into its own. When the all-powerful king of heaven was to set up his reign, it was not necessary for the people of this king to cooperate with others outside the circle of believers. In fact, it seemed imperative to avoid any contact except that calculated to persuade outsiders to become members of the sect. This was in keeping with the eschatological vision. Frequently, the new age pictured all men adopting the religion of Israel. The event of judgment implied that only true believers would be permitted to enjoy the blessings of the Kingdom.

I submit that the ethic of process eschatology will need to adopt a different attitude toward religious commitment and toward membership in a religious community. The goals of Jesus' eschatology, even after adjustment for man's responsibility in history as process, are too grand in scope ever to be achieved by believers alone. In the older view, participation in the new world depended upon remaining aloof from this world. The newer view requires cooperation with others or there will be very little Kingdom for anyone to enjoy. Cooperation requires that the church learn to respect the efforts and motives of other agents of helpful social change. This does not mean that the religious person need hide the religious dimension of his own motivation. It does mean that he will need to be able to advocate the church's strategy and tactics for increasing the well-being of the race on nonreligious grounds, which should be easy since he is working for the well-being of men and not merely the enhancement of the status of the religious community. This does, however, imply a God less jealous of recognition than the traditional view suggests. We shall have to return to this theme. Here we are concerned with the full implication of a social eschatology for an eschatological ethic.

Responsibility for bringing to pass the analogous equivalents of the older end of the world make the newer ethic a social ethic in two special senses. It is a way of life for a community because only groups have power to effect the kind of change necessary. We have called it a strategy and tactic because it is designed to guide a group to influence the shape of the life of society.

This also means that it must be an ethic designed by a group. In the older view, ethical direction was given by authority through a spokesman who displayed the credentials of a man of God. In the newer view, group consensus plays the same role as authority did in the older one. The procedure any particular congregation of believers uses to achieve consensus will depend on the models for group decision that inform their other community activities. The ethic of strategy for action that results from group deliberation and decision would then be binding on individual members. In the measure that the group had decided that certain kinds of action were important to the purpose of the congregation, to that extent individual freedom is suspended. This subordination of the individual to the group would be the analogous equivalent of obedience in the older view.

The ethic thus devised would be a religious ethic because of the common conviction that constituted the group. Jesus provides the supreme declaration of what human life ought to be. The ethic would not be a simple repetition of Jesus' teaching. Much of Jesus' ethic would be directly usable, but since his ethic was not designed to inform a program of social change, the new ethic will need to incorporate elements that never occurred to Jesus. The directly applicable aspects of Jesus' ethical teaching will tend to be those which deal with private existence relatively independent of the community. But care must be taken to avoid perpetuating ethical imperatives that seem important only as prerequisites to entrance into the Kingdom. Enough energy has been wasted achieving higher levels of virtue and righteousness for their own sakes. On the other hand, too high a premium often has been put upon absolute individual ethical freedom with the result that it becomes extremely difficult for Protestants to mobilize for social ends. Too often the adventurous are not clear enough about what they are free for or they are reluctant to risk their newfound freedom in communal commitment.

But what can guide the church beyond Jesus' ethic to a more relevant one? This question leads us to see in what sense the church's ethic by being eschatological sooner or later comes to the end of religion. To develop an analogous vision of the better world worth living for, the church receives a certain value orientation from its tradition. This is not enough to complete the vision. Behavioral sciences in historical perspective must be allowed to have the most to say about what is likely to be good for man and about what means are likely to lead toward those goals which the traditional vision of the Kingdom embodied. The ethics of traditional eschatology provide preliminary guidelines and an accompanying critique of developing goals and programs, but research in behavioral sciences must provide the substance of the ethics of process eschatology.

We have observed elsewhere that an overemphasis upon the chronology of eschatological fulfillment in the New Testament has obscured the question about the scope of eschatology. But once the worldwide, social, communal scope has been recovered, then chronological considerations may be allowed to have their proper cogency. "When will these things be?" the disciples asked. The implication was that the really important things were in the future. It has been the service of people like Dodd, Kümmel, and lately Perrin to call attention to the synoptic sayings that put a measure of the blessing of the Kingdom in the present. This partial enjoyment of life was tolerable when it was possible to guarantee a future epoch of complete blessedness in which true believers were assured a share. But when the process eliminates this kind of epoch, the decisive epoch becomes the life-span of any particular person. It would be no loving service of man's well-being to continue to place the fullest enjoyment of life in some future he would never live to see. Just as the static eschatology taught its devotee to savor the life of the future, so process eschatology teaches its pupils to savor the present for all it is worth for as long as it lasts, even while engaged in efforts to provide the rising generation with a more savory present in its time.

It will seem to some that the result of our hermeneutic of analogy is too humanistic, too preoccupied with man, and too little concerned with God to be an adequate equivalent to the religion of tradition. In the past, this criticism has been enough to dispose of explorations like this one. But such criticism misses the seriousness of the problem modern convictional structures pose. Simple repetition of a traditional view is conceptually impossible. To condemn the kind of possibility we have been exploring is to condemn increasing numbers of people to alienation from Christian tradition. And as I have maintained, this is not fair since it refuses to recognize the cultural relativity of all religious convictional structures including the traditional, normative one. Although the religious structure we have been exploring works out to a kind of humanitarianism, this does not automatically reduce its religious value.

The complaint about being too humanitarian must really be an expression of dissatisfaction with the role assigned to God. I can only reiterate that God as the all-wise declarer of the true destiny of man by his decisive word on the subject, Jesus of Nazareth, the eschatological prophet, is the most important conceivable person that our modern convictional structure can posit. To believe that Jesus was God's last word and that God continues to persuade men to serve the destiny declared in Jesus is the keystone of the existence of such a believer. Not to credit him with true religion is to miss completely the conditions under which conviction forms. Compare our suggested form of faith with a convictional structure that has no role at all for God and we come closer to the crux of today's hermeneutical problem.

It is not uncommon to find people who share the values of the convictional structure of the modern pilgrim we have been describing, but who are quite puzzled by any role for God. There are no doubt many reasons for this very real puzzlement —one of the chief being, perhaps, that most of the people they have known heretofore who "believe in God" have not seemed to be committed to a relevant or civilized application of love and justice. The other main reason is less subjective. As moderns, committed to a relatively consistent empiricism, they have found it necessary to discard the idealistic tradition stemming from Plato. Gods and absolute ideals have simply lost reality status along with the whole realm of the ideal. For, in the empirical setting of their convictional world, the ideal realm that was primary before has now become a shadowy, questionable derivative one. This being the case, a God who is by tradition a spirit and resides there, simply has no place.

This is the perspective that brings conventional hermeneutics to its limits. The New Testament does not anticipate this convictional situation. Denial of the existence of God in the New Testament could only be an act of sinful rebellion. At best, it might be a temporary state that sooner or later would be invaded by irrefutable evidence to the effect not only that God exists but also that he reigns. Now the situation is completely different. Today's apparently "godless" pilgrim has nothing against God. He is not in rebellion against him. He just cannot let such a being be and still make sense of reality. He can recognize the necessity of a God figure for others as a supportive psychological mechanism, but he cannot grant this helpful mechanism the ontological status of a particular, distinct being.

Suppose this pilgrim does have great respect for Jesus and the church. Jesus is for him *the* great exponent of the best values of Western civilization. It is his conviction that if we could interpret these ideals for our daily life as effectively as Jesus did for his day, then we would be fulfilling our obligation to our time. Insofar as the church works for the social change and style of life that Jesus' teaching requires, this pilgrim wants to share in the undertaking. What relation has his convictional structure to the conventional one?

There is no question that the relation is complicated by the elimination of a role for God. But there is no use wishing our postreligion pilgrim would rework his convictional structure to make a place for God. We must allow in his case the same integral relation between religious convictions and all his other convictions that we have assumed in the major illustration.

If we were successful in getting our inquirer to add on religious convictions about God which he would have to set aside in his ordinary life, there would certainly be no gain for God or religion. In fact, it could conceivably be more advan-

tageous to a man to come to the realization that belief in God
had little meaning for him than to continue an empty affirma-
tion that has little operational value. Nonfunctional religious
convictions can only be a burden that saps life instead of sup-
porting it. Suppose then we allow our postreligious pilgrim the
dictates of his convictions, that is, no place for God. The difference between him and the early Christian is striking, to say
the least. Are there important similarities that might conceivably justify an equivalent status?

The most obvious similarity is the commitment to the same
goal for humanity that results from a common admiration of
the teaching of Jesus. The main difference is that this goal is
grounded in God for the conventionally religious and is self-
validating for our "godless" pilgrim. Mankind has intrinsic
worth to this modern. Put another way, to love one's neighbor
is simply to acknowledge in others the same value one recognizes in oneself as a human being.

But what about the persuasive role for God as the one who
steadies a man in his ambivalent and fitful recognition of his
own and others' worth? This role could be filled by a community of men committed to the same goal. All members of
such a community are not likely to be overwhelmed by ambivalence or to lose their identity at the same moment. And there
are always the models of men from the past who did persevere.
This supportive role of a community of like-minded men
explains the desire of this person to be related to the church in
spite of its religion. His desire for community has its functional
equivalent in the church. Jesus as a steadying model from the
past is a functional equivalent for Christology. Naturally,
Jesus in this role cannot be ontologically unique by virtue of
having both a divine and human nature since this convictional
structure has no place for divine nature. Instead Jesus becomes
the most important among other important models. This is as
close an equivalent as this convictional structure can manage,
indeed the only equivalent possible in a convictional setting
without ontological levels, that is, without the other world.

This disregard of God is a stumbling block for the religious person to whom God is the most important being on the scene. The traditionally religious person, of course, must continue to believe that God exists and, in the face of the form of faith I have suggested, to wonder how God may feel about his eclipse. Tradition makes him a jealous God who will not be ignored. Again, we must ask about convictional models from ordinary experience imported to give new shape to the amorphous God of the Second Commandment.

A god jealous of the recognition justly due him connotes a king upon whose glory the security of his realm in large measure depends. Much in the Biblical tradition respects this model. But tradition also points another way. Jesus achieved glory through humility and recommended this path to believers. Does not this imply that God is willing to take this way? If we shift the model from king to father, we are in a better position to understand the self-effacing side of the Biblical tradition about God.

In a modern convictional context, the maturity of a child depends at certain points on rejecting or disregarding his father in order for the child to become a person in his own right. It will not be surprising if a world come of age produces men who, for a time, need to forget their heavenly father to reach fuller maturity as his children. Those who find it possible and important to posit God will hope this loss of a place for God may turn out to be temporary. But until post-God pilgrims do recover a viable way to believe in God, a hermeneutic of analogy suggests that they ought not be treated as prodigals who are acceptable only after they come to themselves and return to their father.

There is a mystery in this new form of ungodliness as fascinating as the mystery of traditional godliness. God-oriented pilgrims perhaps should explain their godless co-pilgrims as evidence of God's mysterious powers of persuasion. Jesus' use of the Samaritan and Paul's use of Gentiles as models for godliness superior to those who believe correctly provide adequate justification in tradition for a new status for "unbelieving" pilgrims.

If this is a fair estimate of the church-oriented, humanitarian, no-God pilgrims, it follows that the church perhaps should find a way to incorporate them into its life and work without compromising their integrity with entrance vows and sacramental commitments. On their part, these pilgrims perhaps can find ways of interpreting prayer and worship as occasion to examine and renew their commitment to the more humane life the church seeks to enjoy and spread, rather than as threats to the integrity of their view of reality.

This illustration of the way of a hermeneutic of analogy might work is the main argument for its validity. But it may help to specify its possible advantages over other suggestions currently being explored.

Compared to Bultmann's demythologizing, the hermeneutic of analogy allows the Biblical images to maintain their full stature. One mistake the liberal tradition has made has been to wish too fervently that the Biblical authors might say exactly what needs to be said today. It is the same error in reverse of the traditionalists who wish too fervently that the Biblical message might be the exact word we ought to pronounce now. It is the hermeneutical mistake of expecting simple correspondence between Biblical good news and good news for today.

Basic to this mistake is the supposition that the religious convictions of Jesus and the earliest church were unrelated to the rest of the convictions of their cultures. The world of that time had a unified convictional structure where religious and extra-religious convictions were in simple harmony. Each realm informed the other. The hermeneutic of analogy hopes to recover this wholeness by allowing contemporary secular convictions in each pocket of culture the same free play in the religious sphere as obtained originally.

This has two advantages. First, it opens the way for hermeneutics to take into account the whole range of man's existence and not merely some segment of his life which a particular brand of reformation tradition, existentialism, or linguistic analysis finds significant. It invites wholeness beyond the crippling schizophrenia of secular and sacred. Second, it frees our religious heritage to participate in and contribute to the invention and pursuit of a larger life for man under God. We have hoped to suggest a civilized and civilizing hermeneutic and one that offers a viable way to believe now what other people of God have believed in their time.

NOTES

1. Willem F. Zuurdeeg, *An Analytical Philosophy of Religion* (Abingdon Press, 1958).

2. Here I include the Bultmannian school, van Buren and Ebeling.

3. Harvey Cox, *The Secular City* (The Macmillan Company, 1965).

4. Van Harvey, *The Historian and the Believer* (The Macmillan Company, 1966).

5. B. S. Childs, *Memory and Tradition in Israel* (London: SCM Press, Ltd., 1962).

6. *Ibid.*, p. 85.